Migration:

Multiculturalism and its Metaphors

Theodore Dalrymple

Connor Court Publishing

Published in 2016 by Connor Court Publishing Pty Ltd

Connor Court Publishing Pty Ltd
PO Box 7257
Redland Bay QLD 4165
sales@connorcourt.com
www.connorcourt.com
Phone 0497-900-685

ISBN: 978-1-925501-10-0

Cover design: Maria Giordano

Photo © Vicheslav, istockphoto

Printed in Australia

To the memories of Paddy McGuinness and Roddy Meagher.

Also to the memory of Nicholas Packham, a surgeon who invited me out to Australia years ago.

Foreword

Migration realists might have hoped the terror of the November 2015 Paris terrorist attack, combined with horrors of the sexual mass-assaults in Cologne and other parts of Europe on New Year's Eve 2016, would prompt a clear-eyed reexamination of the principles and practice of multiculturalism. They might also have hoped—even expected—for this to encompass a reconsideration of the merits of the widely-applauded open borders migration policy implemented by German Chancellor Angela Merkel, which has led to an estimated one million refugees flooding into Germany from Muslim countries in the Middle East and North Africa.

But not even 'events' as shocking as these appear sufficient to knock the conventional political discourse off track and spur second thoughts about the multicultural ideology that says greater diversity is always a good thing and all cultures are equal—contradictory though these claims are. The lesson that should have been well and truly learned by the political classes in the developed world is that the crucial issue in relation to migration and multiculturalism should always be this: what do the newcomers think about the norms and values of the countries they enter, and therefore what are the prospects for successful integration?

The national interest—especially the safety and security of 'native' populations—should come first, and qualify even legitimate humanitarian concerns. Migration and multiculturalism must be dealt with in a hard-headed fashion, or else we will deal with the world the way we want it to be, rather than how it really is. Unfortunately, it takes a lot of reality to overcome the pejoratively ideological habits of mind that are as powerful as those surrounding migration and multiculturalism.

The resilience of orthodox thinking on these topics—the Australian Government's success in 'stopping the boats' notwithstanding—was demonstrated during the 2016 Australian federal election. There was relatively scant debate and controversy (beyond generic electoral barbs about jobs and welfare) generated by the Australian Greens proposals to lift Australia's annual refugee intake to 50,000 souls, with a large percentage of the additional refugees to be taken in from crisis-ridden Iraq and Syria.

The reasons why migration and multicultural ideologies are proving so impenetrable to challenge by reason and logic, despite the plethora of confounding events that ought to clarify thoughts and stiffen wills to avoid disaster, are suggested in this collection of essays by Theodore Dalrymple. Across a range of subjects—from Germanine Greer's mau-mauing about Aboriginality, to the deeper meaning of Michel Houellebecqu's *Submission*, to Pope Francis's impractical moralising on refugees drowning at sea, to the politically correct outrage prompted by a Bill Leak cartoon—Dalrymple explores how contemporary delusions about migration and multiculturalism are underpinned by two of the most powerful social sentiments in modern western societies.

The first is the determination among political, media, and academic elites to oppose anything that even hints at lapsing into the secular sin of racism. The second is the corresponding desire to appear unquestionably compassionate towards every 'other', irrespective of colour, creed, and nationality. This conspicuous "moral exhibitionism" on matters of race is driven in equal parts by the elites' self-loathing attitudes towards their own societies, and by the desire to distinguish themselves as an educated and enlightened class apart from ordinary citizens presumed morally inferior and prejudiced by default.

These essays illuminate these motivations so well in part because the author tells us how he shares the best part of these sympathies, and in the resulting "moral dilemma". Having met assorted, and usually gainfully-employed, refugees (and economic migrants who have entered Europe illegally) Dalrymple tells us it is impossible not to admire and feel for the plight of individuals who have escaped from repressive political regimes, and who are willing to work hard to improve their own and their family's material well-being.

But as we would expect of the great chronicler of the destructive social impact of the welfare state on the morals and manners of modern Britain, Dalrymple brings his trademark powers of cultural observation to the real analytical task: assessing the aggregate social, political, and economic effects of migration and multiculturalism. Where ideology and sentimentalism are pled in the name of migration and multiculturalism, this collection characteristically calls out nonsense and humbug, and elucidates the discomforting truths that too many construe with blind-eyes.

The full force of Dalrymple's intellect and erudition is turned on those whose muddled minds and bleeding hearts won't allow them to look in the face the realities that belie their preferred modes of thought. The message and implication of these essays is that those who want to valorise cultural difference, and yet wish to assume that all peoples from all cultures have the same values, hopes, and aspirations, cannot have what Dalrymple calls — to adapt a metaphor—their "cultural minestrone" and eat it too.

Jeremy Sammut
Senior Research Fellow
The Centre for Independent Studies
May 2016

Introduction

For most people, I suspect, multiculturalism means a lot of different restaurants: which, I surmise, explains why the doctrine has made such deep inroads into the Anglo-Saxon world with its relatively impoverished culinary traditions. What multiculturalism decidedly does *not* mean is a serious interest in the cultures of other peoples, for foreign languages are difficult to learn and foreign customs difficult to understand.

Nor, when understood, will they necessarily be approved of: and no one in his right mind would want to introduce Somalian or Cambodian political traditions into Australia. Let us at least have no humbug.

There is, however, no subject on which so much humbug is talked, written or broadcast as on immigration. This is understandable, because the whole question is fraught with difficulties from which the mind, ever in the search for easy solutions, averts itself. Nasty xenophobia on the one hand confronts lazy liberalism on the other. Difficult questions such as the conflict between the national interest and humanitarian feeling are assiduously avoided because they arouse too much anxiety. It is much easier and more gratifying to sink into a nice warm mental bath of self-righteousness.

I do not pretend to have the answer (supposing there is one) to the question of mass migration in the twenty-first century, obviously one of the first importance for a country like Australia, as it is for Europe. In general prudence is a political virtue, but excessive fear also has its dangers. All I can recommend is that we look at reality in the face before we make any decisions whose consequences will stretch far into the future, and this I have tried to do in various articles collected in this short book.

I thank Jeremy Sammut for his preface and Anthony Cappello of Connor Court for suggesting this book. I hope it will cause people to think, even where it does not please them.

Fantasies under the river gums

Review of *Whitefella Jump Up:*
The Shortest Way to Nationhood by Germaine Greer

Just as vulgarity can sometimes transcend itself and
become something else (I am thinking of Gillray and
Las Vegas), so silliness can sometimes transcend itself
and attain sociological significance.

Germaine Greer has written a transcendently silly pamphlet
about a proposed future for her homeland, Australia. She wants
it to become what she calls an Aboriginal Republic, though the
exact meaning of this term is unclear even to her, which is not
altogether surprising, since Aborigines lived in stateless societies
before the arrival of the Europeans. However, her mind is so
completely stocked with clichés that she often uses words that
have connotation but no denotation, as a kind of shorthand. For
example, she suggests that Australia should become a hunter-
gatherer society, presumably because hunter-gatherers are assumed
by the modern right-thinker to be environmentally friendly and at
one with the beneficent vibrations of the cosmos. No concrete
suggestion is forthcoming as to how the five million Sydneysiders,
for example, are to transform themselves into a bow-and-arrow
brigade, living on assorted roots, grubs and game. Of course, like
all great conurbations, Sydney already has its hunter-gatherers:

they're called burglars and robbers, but I don't suppose this is what she meant.

She thinks that Australia as an Aborigine Republic could make common cause in the United Nations with other formerly colonised countries. It would thereby join the ranks of victim states, thus achieving the moral purity of, say, Idi Amin's Uganda, Hafaz Assad's Syria or Ne Win's Burma.

Greer's Australia, to whose problems her constitutional vapourings are supposedly the answer, is a place unrecognisable to me, and seems to exist largely in her fantasies. For her, it is a continent utterly ruined by rapacity and colonised by none but crude alcoholics, who have created a society of which nothing good whatever can be said. This society has only destroyed; it has created or built nothing of any value. Its inhabitants are wretched, sobering up only to inject themselves with drugs in order to sink back into unconsciousness or to commit suicide. They aren't even prosperous, working, according to her, for a miserable pittance.

Strange, then, that half the world should wish to migrate there, despite the fact that Australia is, in Greer's view, deplorably monoglot instead of being laudably polyglot. If only Australians would learn Pushtu, Spanish, Farsi, Italian, Cambodian, Kurdish, Greek, Arabic, Russian, Chinese and Tamil, instead of so intolerantly sticking to English! Mind you, on her view of Australian society, any attempts to keep refugees out must be considered laudable, for it is preserving them from the living hell they will find if they get there.

Luckily for Australia, according to Greer, a solution to the alleged impasse created by this loathsome society is at hand: the noble savage. Australians should recognise what she calls, without troubling the reader with anything as crude as a definition, their 'aboriginality'. What is certain is that all goodness, wisdom, culture and knowledge inhere in the Aborigines. They are so spiritual, in fact, that Greer has only to sit with them 'on my mattress under the river gums' (why the mattress, one might ask, in one so aboriginal?) to 'feel all around me a new kind of consciousness in which self was subordinate to awelye, the interrelationship of everything, skin, earth, language'. Gosh, the Aborigines were able to subdue Greer's sense of self! There must be something to them after all.

This kind of insincere and highly derivative drivel—the Australian equivalent of Marie Antoinette playing at shepherdess —is not without interest, for it tells us quite a lot about the soul of modern man. It is not self-hatred, exactly, for not even her worst enemies would accuse Greer of that: rather, it is a kind of moral exhibitionism, a claim of superiority to all those who haven't communed with the Aboriginal Brahman on mattresses under river gums and who have instead made lives for themselves in Sydney or Melbourne.

Actually, I think Greer may be right to point to an existential unease common in Australia, but it is certainly not an unease unique to Australia. We now have societies in which quite large numbers of people have no religious belief, no interest in the life of the mind, and no struggle for survival. For them, the difference in reward between working very hard and not working at all is not great. What, then, can engage their minds or impassion them, apart from personal crises of their own making? That is why self-destructive social pathology is so prevalent, but not just in Australia.

I suspect that what infuriates Australian intellectuals about Australia is their profound irrelevance to their own society, thanks to the fact that Australia is about as good as modern, large-scale human societies get. Australia can easily confront man with the irreducible discontents of human existence, once his desires have been met, discontents which intellectuals are powerless to assuage.

The Russian model of the intelligentsia, as being the bearers of a providential historical role, has exerted a baleful influence on the imagination of western intellectuals ever since the Russian revolution at least. Unlike a Russian exile such as Herzen, however, Greer is of no real importance. This is her scream of protest.

The Spectator, 3 July 2004

An Imaginary Scandal

If a prisoner walks into my consulting room in the prison with a stick, he's a sex offender; if he has gold front teeth, he's a drug dealer; and if he's reading Wittgenstein, he's in for fraud: for it is virtually a law of our penal establishments that fraud and philosophy are what literary theorists like to call metonymic.

When you work in a prison as I do, white-collar criminals come as something of a light relief. At last someone with whom you can have a disinterested, abstract intellectual conversation! No more talk about alcoholic mothers, brutal stepfathers, and terrible childhoods as the *fons et origo* of car theft: it's straight to the meaning of life, the social contract and the metaphysical foundation of morality (they always say that there isn't any). It's almost like being a student again, up till three in the morning, trying to work out what no man has ever worked out before.

The fact is that people who commit fraud, at least on a large scale, have lively, intelligent minds. I usually end up admiring them, despite myself. My last encounter was with a man who defrauded the government of $38,000,000 of value added tax. I am afraid that I laughed. After all, he had merely united customers with cheap goods. Unfortunately for him, he had been lifted from his tropical paradise hideaway by helicopter and then extradited. By the time I met him, though, his sentence was almost over. He had discovered Wittgenstein in prison.

"Did you have to pay the money back?" I asked.

"No," he replied, "though I would have had a shorter sentence if I had."

He had calculated that an extra two years as a guest of Her Majesty was worth it. I shook his hand, as a man who was unafraid: I could do no other.

I feel more or less the same about literary fraud (I am, of course, talking of the fully conscious variety, not the other kind, which is far too commonplace to be interesting). We all have our favorites in this genre: Napoleon liked his Ossian, but my favorite is Rahila Khan. She deserves to be more widely known than she is, for ultimately her fraud was no fraud.

Her oeuvre is very slender: a single paperback volume of 100 pages, entitled *Down the Road, Worlds Away*. It was published in 1987 by the Virago Press, a feminist publishing house founded in the 1970s that is now owned by TimeWarnerBooks, and it appeared in a series called Virago Upstarts—that is to say, parvenu termagants. You are never too young to resent.

"Virago Upstarts is a new series of books for girls and young women... This new series will show the funny, difficult, and exciting real lives and times of teenage girls in the 1980s." No prizes for guessing the reality of the real lives, of course: and Rahila Khan gives us "twelve haunting stories about Asian girls and white boys ... about the tangle of violence and tenderness ... in all their lives," written "with hard-eyed realism and poignant simplicity."

As for Rahila herself, she was born in Coventry in 1950, lived successively in Birmingham, Derby, Oxford, London, and Peterborough, married in 1971, and now lived in Brighton with her two daughters. She began writing only in 1986 (presumably when her daughters demanded less of her time), and in the same year six of her stories were broadcast by the BBC. Virago accepted her book, an acceptance that, in the words of Professor Dympna Callaghan, Professor of English at Syracuse University and author of a Marxist analysis of the exclusion of women from the Renaissance stage, "seemed to fulfill one of Virago's laudable objectives, that of publishing the work of a diverse group of contemporary feminist authors."

A literary agent contacted Rahila Khan by post and asked to represent her. Until then, Miss Khan had refused to meet in person anyone with whom she dealt, or even to send a photograph of herself: but she agreed to meet the agent who wanted to represent her. The agent was surprised to discover that Miss Khan was actually the Reverend Toby Forward, a Church of England vicar. (He has recently been installed as canon residentiary and preceptor of Liverpool Cathedral, and his latest publication—he is now an established children's writer under his own name—is entitled *Shakespeare's Globe: An Interactive Pop-Up Theatre.*)

Needless to say, the revelation of Rahila Khan's true identity caused both hilarity and anger. The publisher, Virago, felt that it had been made a fool of and was the victim of a distasteful hoax, pulped the book soon after its publication and turned it into an expensive bibliographical rarity (my own copy is in excellent condition but for the yellowing pages that emit an acrid, throat-catching smell which so many British books, printed on the cheapest and nastiest of paper, nowadays emit after a few months of existence). Virago asked Reverend Forward to return the advance he had been paid and to pay for the cost of the printing. He did not accede to the request.

Virago felt it necessary to stand by its purely literary judgment, namely that the stories were written "with hard-eyed realism and poignant simplicity"—it had to do so, or it would justly have been accused of applying double standards to work by Asian women and white men, which would have revealed a frankly racist condescension. But Virago decided that politics in this instance was the better part of literature, and was more important, indeed, than whether the book had anything worthwhile or important to say. It therefore refused to sell any more copies of the offending work. This, as we shall see, was ironic, because the author was drawing attention, not before time, to the truly oppressed condition of certain women, a condition in which one might have supposed that feminists would be interested. The personal identity of the author thus came to be all-important just at the very moment when, elsewhere in the literary world, the death of the author was being confidently announced.

Academics and intellectuals found the affair painful to elucidate. If it were true that the balkanization of literature was justified by the supposition that only people who belonged to a certain category of people could truly understand, write about, interpret, and sympathize with the experiences of people in that same category, so that, for example, only women could write about women for women, and only blacks about blacks for blacks (the very careers of many academics now depending upon such a supposition), how was it possible that a Church of England vicar had been able, actually without much difficulty, to persuade a feminist publishing house that he wrote as a woman, and as a Muslim woman of Indian subcontinental origin at that? Was he not in fact telling us, as presumably a good Christian should, that mankind is essentially one, and that if we make a sufficient effort we too can enter into the worlds of others who are in many ways different from ourselves?

Was he not implying that the traditional view of literature, that it expresses the universal in the particular, was not only morally and religiously superior, but empirically a more accurate description of it as an enterprise than the view of literature as a series of stockades, from which groups of the embittered and enraged endlessly fired arrows at one another without ever quite achieving victory?

The confusion that the affair sowed was evident in the clotted prose that it stimulated. Here is Professor Callaghan again in her essay, "The Vicar and Virago":

> As we saw in the Vicar and Virago Affair, the problem of identity is exacerbated to the point of hypervisibility in the relation between the cultural inscription of race as color and the erasure of race in the dominant construction of white identity. Whites are feverishly clutching at their/ our ethnicities—and everyone else's—and are threatened by the knowledge that the racially hegemonic invisibility so long cultivated may now spell disappearance. In its worst manifestations, this becomes neo-Nazism, but even at its best, this attempt to register whiteness as a racial identity risks reproducing the notion of race as an objective (rather than socially constructed) spectrum of human identity. "Equalizing" racial categories will only succeed in suspending the history of racism and making whiteness, as opposed to white privilege, visible.

The great advantage that Reverend Forward enjoyed over his publishers and critics was that he knew what he was talking about and they didn't. His critics probably assumed that, as a vicar of the national church in seemingly terminal decline, he was an otherworldly scion of the English country gentry in its last gasp, who could therefore be expected not to know much about anything, and was at best a figure of fun. But from the moment I started to read the stories in Down the Road, Worlds Away (and the title itself should have given a clue to the book's serious intent, capturing in five words a very important element of modern social reality), I understood that the author was not in any sense perpetrating a hoax, much less a fraud. He was writing in earnest, and not satirizing anyone. For what he described in his stories was only too familiar to me from my work as a doctor, and no one could write so clearly of such matters without a deep sense of purpose.

The Reverend Toby Forward, as it happens, is not the scion of privilege, even of privilege in decline; his biography in outline followed that of Rahila Khan's very closely. He was born in Coventry in 1950, and did live for many years in the cities of the English Midlands. He did marry in 1971, did have two daughters, did start to write in 1986, and did live in Brighton at the time the book was published.

The Reverend Forward's knowledge of the kind of people I have been treating as a doctor for many years came to him by a different route from my knowledge of them. It so happens that I have worked in the very same area that the Reverend Forward writes about, where his father was a publican. Both his parents, who were working class, left school when they were fourteen years old. They lived in slum areas of the unlovely cities of the Midlands, and he himself went to schools in which half the pupils were of Indian or Pakistani descent. His early life was lived in precisely the social environment depicted in Down the Road, Worlds Away: that is to say, in a society in which a nihilistic and entirely secular white working-class culture was thrown into involuntary contact with a besieged traditionalist Indian culture in which religion, particularly Islam, played a preponderant role.

Oddly enough for a book supposedly by someone called Rahila Khan, the five stories about white boys are narrated in the first person, while the seven about Muslim girls are in the third person. The editor at Virago solicitously (and by letter) "wondered whether this represented your feelings about the place of Asian women particularly in Britain, that the sense of 'otherness' is still so great that it feels still an impossibility to write in first person as opposed to third."

Now that we know the true identity of Rahila Khan, the explanation is rather clearer. The Reverend Forward had experienced the life of white working-class nihilism himself, and was therefore able to depict it in the first person, while his depiction of the life of the Muslim girls was based on close observation and imaginative inference. Interestingly, however, no one criticized Rahila Khan, while she was still thought to be a Muslim woman, for having written about the lives of white working-class boys.

The stories about the boys reveal a world in which high intelligence is a disadvantage and even a danger. Having no vision of a better life instilled at home, and being given none by a society that has now all but officially adopted an ideology that refuses to recognize a higher and a lower among human activities and aspirations, young boys who possess intelligence and spirit are driven to rebellion in a wholly destructive and self-destructive way. The narrator of the stories loves his mother, but only his mother, and she soon dies of cancer, after which he is unable to approach the rest of the world other than with violent bravado. In one story, he attends a clandestine dog-fight that symbolizes the brutality of life in a British slum, a fight that is described by the vicar with such terrifying clarity that one assumes it is a memory rather than an invention. The final story narrated by the white youth concerns a car thief, Mickey Singh (a Sikh who has thrown in his lot with the white working-class "culture"), who lets a young neophyte called Patch drive a car he has stolen. Patch is so called because he has a black patch over his eye to cure his squint, and is (possibly as a consequence) a weakling in a social environment in which weakness or any kind of disability is mercilessly mocked and exploited—and who therefore wants to steal a car to prove himself. He crashes the car and is killed. Mickey Singh, who survives unscathed, is sent to prison, where the narrator visits him.

> They shouldn't have put him in prison. Not just for taking cars, not even after Patch died. I went to visit him. He was different. He looked good. He was calm and relaxed. I don't know. He seemed to have got something. Usually if I want something I go out and get it, but I don't really know what I want yet. But Mickey, he's got something he wants, now, and I want that.

The doom of an entire class, composed of millions of people, is most sensitively captured here (for, significantly, it is the last word of the white youth that we read in the book). The "just" of "not just for taking cars" is absolutely accurate: my patients in the prison often say "just for cars" when I ask them why they are in prison. The narrator's admiration for Mickey, and desire to be like him, is also entirely accurate. In the area in which I work, quite a few young people tattoo themselves with a blue spot on the cheek to make it appear that they have been incarcerated in young offenders' institutions, whose inmates tattoo themselves in this fashion, even though they have never been so incarcerated. For them, though, the blue spot is a badge of honor, and moreover a talisman in an environment in which toughness is the highest good and tenderness and solicitousness for others mere weakness. With neither sanctimony nor censoriousness, the vicar succeeds in condemning a heartless way of life, in which other people are but instruments to be used for short-term material or sensual advantage, a way of life that has no charms and has nothing whatever to be said in its favor.

The vicar's understanding of the tragic world of Muslim girls living in British slums, caught between two cultures and belonging fully to neither, possessing little power to determine their own fates, seems to me to be equally accurate. Indeed, he explores this world with considerable subtlety as well as sympathy.

The girls are vastly superior, morally and intellectually, to their white counterparts. Their problem is precisely the opposite of that of the white youths: far from nihilism, it is the belief in a code of ethics and conduct so rigid that it makes no allowances for the fact that the girls have grown up and must live in a country with a very different culture from that of the country in which their parents grew up. In the eyes of their parents, the girls are easily infected with, or corrupted by, the dream of personal freedom, and since the only result of such personal freedom that the parents see around them is the utter disintegration of the white working class into fecklessness and slovenly criminality, where every child is a bastard and families are kaleidoscopic in their swiftly changing composition, they become even more rigidly conservative than they might otherwise have been. They cling to what they know, as to a plank in a storm at sea.

The fathers of the girls are good according to their own lights; they are kindly and loving, but not unconditionally so. The condition of their continuing affection for their daughters is automatic, unthinking obedience. The girls are brought up in a micro-totalitarianism, in which everything that is not forbidden is compulsory. Since such a system is strong but rigid and brittle, the slightest sign of disobedience, or even independence of thought, is treated as a serious danger signal, that if allowed to go unpunished could destroy the whole culture.

In one of the stories, a father who had hitherto been kindly to his daughter, Amina, showers blows on her when he discovers that she has a book by D. H. Lawrence in her bag, given her to read by her English teacher after she has expressed an interest in literature.

Her father complains to the school about the teacher's conduct, and the headmaster replies to him in a pusillanimously emollient way. But Amina continues to admire and be grateful to the English teacher, who "at least ... was one person who knew how she felt and who respected her."

The story ends tragically, however, when she overhears him talking to another teacher near the end of the school term.

"Only a few days, thank God. What a hellish term."

"Glad it's over?" his colleague had asked, with little real interest.

"Fifth form lessons are always a pain. Most of them never want to learn. D'you know, this year I nearly got the sack." And he began the tale of Amina and the book. As he told it, the colleague's interest became genuine.

"Why did you do it?" the other teacher asked at last. "These Paki girls never come to anything. It's a waste of time sticking your neck out."

In a tragic and terrible moment, Amina realizes that she can expect no real help from white society, while she is completely alienated from her own. She is alone in the whole world, but without any means to cope. The story helps us to feel for ourselves her hermetic isolation in a crowded world.

This passage, in my view, demonstrates that the Church of England vicar (the very term arouses sniggers in the intelligentsia) has understood something important, because he is concerned for the welfare of people other than himself, whom self-aggrandizing middle-class feminists still consider to be below their august notice. It is not optimistic in a facile way, because the teacher's observation, that "these Paki girls never come to anything," is all too often accurate, in that it recognizes both their superior potential and the social pressure on them that prevents them from coming to anything. Quite apart from anything else, *Down the Road, Worlds Away* confronts intellectuals with an uncomfortable truth: you can't be a multiculturalist and believe in the legal equality of the sexes. To deal with the problems of modern society, hard thought, confrontation with an often unpleasant reality, and moral courage are needed, for which a vague and self-congratulatory broadmindedness is no substitute. Think not that the Reverend Forward is come to send complacency among intellectuals, but thought. Oddly enough, they don't seem to like it.

In the subtlest of the stories, "Winter Wind," a Muslim girl called Fatima is allowed by her reluctant father to go with pupils from her school to the theatre, to see a production of *As You Like It*. He allows it only because the play is a set text for her English exam, and Fatima is a good pupil. She looks forward to the play with great anticipation. For her, "it was as exciting as a journey to another world." By now, we realize that this is the literal truth.

In the theatre, she sits next to Colin, a white boy who lacks "the prowess and the personality to make a success in the adolescent world." She communicates her enthusiasm for Shakespeare to him, which is itself both accurate and ironical in its observation. The irony lies in a Pakistani girl conveying a love of Shakespeare to a boy of purely English origin; the accuracy lies in the unfashionable understanding that high culture has a powerfully liberating effect upon the unfree and the downtrodden, which is why the intelligent among them, like Fatima, so powerfully crave it.

Here again, the story does not end on a note of facile optimism. Colin and Fatima become lovers; before long, she is alone in labor in the maternity ward. We assume that by now Colin has lost interest in her, and all her father's apprehensions about allowing her to go to the theatre—a symbol for Westernization—turn out to have been justified. In effect, she has joined the white underclass of single mothers, to whom she is morally and intellectually superior, and without being white. Once again, the fate of a Muslim girl torn between a fundamentally indifferent West and an uncomprehending, unforgiving East is not an enviable one. And of course, her father will not interpret the fulfillment of his worst fears to have been the natural consequence of his own rigid adherence to the traditions he tried to impose on her in an alien land.

This is all uncannily accurate: I have seen it many times in my own hospital. Indeed, I have seen far worse things, tragedies to break the heart. My young Muslim patients, for example, all know of girls who have been killed by their own fathers and brothers when they refused to accede to a forced marriage to their first cousin back home, or to a man four times their age. So why, considering the comparative mildness of the abuses revealed in his stories, did the Reverend Forward feel it necessary to use a pseudonym? For that's all it was, a pseudonym, not an attempt to make a fool of anyone.

He told me that he resorted to his pseudonym because he did not want to receive letters of rejection in his own name, which would somehow be more wounding to his pride than rejections send to Rahila Khan. But he also realized that Rahila Khan would be more likely to get a hearing than the Reverend Forward, and he felt that he had something important to say that ought to be heard. He had already sent his stories about working-class boys to the BBC under another pseudonym, Tom Dale, while he sent the ones about the Muslim girls as Rahila Khan. The BBC had treated the two writers quite differently: kind and considerate to Rahila, brusque and even rude to Tom. He learned his lesson.

Unfortunately, the ensuing furor over his identity and whether, again in the words of Professor Callaghan, "the appropriation of subordinate identities by privileged whites demonstrates that endeavours to compensate for the exclusion of racial 'minorities' from the means of literary production can become the very means for continuing this exclusion," obscured the importance of what he was trying to say. Indeed, one might even interpret the furor over these matters as a displacement activity of the intelligentsia, who wanted to avoid having to think of the very difficult and real problems that he had raised in his stories, and which are so distressing to contemplate.

A Marxist interpretation of the response to the Reverend Forward's pseudonymous activities (incidentally, he has also written as a gypsy, Judy Delaghty, as well as a book of the replies he received from Anglican bishops when he wrote them spoof letters as Francis Wagstaffe, and published as *The Spiritual Quest of Francis Wagstaffe*) would be as follows: he has demonstrated that it is possible for a person with one identity to enter accurately into the experience of people with quite another identity. Since the existence of so many posts in the humanities departments of our universities depends on precisely the opposite assumption, and since the holders of those posts are so intensely second-rate that they would not otherwise occupy such pleasant billets, it was necessary to obscure the significance of his work by means of an ideological smokescreen. Only thus could the economic interests of the holders of pseudo-academic pseudo-positions be protected. The real fraud was in academia, not in his pseudonymity.

When the Reverend Forward adopts a pseudonym, it is clearly for a serious purpose. We are increasingly unable to make the distinctions between seriousness and earnestness, on the one hand, and lightheartedness and frivolity, on the other. The academics are earnest without being serious, the Reverend Forward lighthearted without being frivolous. I am certain that he is right that we can enter into the experience of other people. I confirm this each time I ask a Muslim patient who is resisting a forced marriage whether her mother has yet thrown herself to the ground and claimed to be dying of a heart attack brought on by disobedience. However miserable my patient may be, she laughs: for this is precisely what her mother has done, and it comes as a great relief to her that someone understands. (Most such patients marry in the end, though, or leave home and are horribly exploited by members of their "community" who consider them little better than prostitutes.)

The Reverend Forward does not make the mistake of believing that his ability to enter into the experience of others is infinite. He said to me that, while he could easily put himself in the place of a girl being forced to marry against her will, he could not put himself in the place of a father who killed his daughter for disobeying him. And then he added that, as the father of two daughters, he could easily enter the experience of a man who killed his daughter's boyfriend.

Humor, fearlessness, seriousness, and honesty: the qualities that are hated with an equal hatred by all the smelly little orthodoxies that are contending for tenure in the humanities departments of our universities. There lies the real literary scandal of our times.

The New Criterion, May 2005

France's

A review of Michel Houellebecq's newest novel
Soumission. Flammarion.

For those disinclined to believe in coincidence, the date of the terrorist attack on Charlie Hebdo, January 7, and that of the publication of Michel Houellebecq's latest novel, *Soumission* (Submission), in which a Muslim is elected President of France, were linked in some unspecified way, though it will now never be known precisely in what way. Certainly the novel had received an enormous amount of publicity before publication, so that almost everyone knew of its central conceit. If the novel is dead, as many have claimed, its ghost is certainly able still to haunt us.

Houellebecq is a writer with a single underlying theme: the emptiness of human existence in a consumer society devoid of religious belief, political project, or cultural continuity in which, moreover, thanks to material abundance and social security, there is no real struggle for existence that might give meaning to the life of millions. Such a society will not allow you to go hungry or to live in the abject poverty that would once have been the reward of idleness, whether voluntary or involuntary. This, in Houellebecq's vision of the world, lends an inspissated pointlessness to all human activity, which becomes nothing more than a scramble for unnecessary consumer goods that confer no happiness or (at best) a distraction from that very emptiness. For Houellebecq, then, intellectual or cultural activity becomes mere soap opera for the more intelligent and educated rather than something of intrinsic importance or value. That is why a university teacher of economics in one of his books describes his work as the teaching of obvious untruths to careerist morons, rather than as, say, the awakening of young minds to the fascinating task of reducing the complexity of social interactions to general principles.

So brilliantly does Houellebecq describe the arduous vacuity of the life of his protagonists that one suspects (or knows?) that his books are strongly autobiographical, not in the shallow sense that the incidents in them are necessarily those that he has lived, but in the deeper sense that the whole of what one might call the feeling-tone of his protagonists is actually his. This tone is in a way worse than mere despair, which has at least the merit of strength and of posing a possible solution, namely suicide; the Houellebeckian mood is as chronic illness is to acute, an ache rather than a pain. In *Soumission,* for example, the protagonist, a university teacher of literature, describes his (and, implicitly by extension, our) daily life as but a succession of trivial, boring problems and imperative tasks that are the dark side, as it were, of modern convenience: "blocked washbasin, internet connection broken, speeding ticket, dishonest cleaning lady, mistake in tax return." I doubt whether there is anybody—any middle class person at any rate—who will be unfamiliar with these irritations that can, if they accumulate, come so easily to dominate our thoughts and to color our attitude to life.

Food and sex partake of the meaninglessness of Houellebecq's world. For example, the microwave is almost the only instrument in his *batterie de cuisine,* and when it fails to heat supermarket-prepared meals he is reduced to hummus and taramasalata or home delivery. As for sex, it is merely an intermittent itch that has to be scratched; it is never the expression of affection, let alone of love, and if by any chance a relation forms between the participants, it is bound either to fizzle out in boredom or end in recrimination. The very ease with which sex can now take place deprives it of any special meaning and turns it purely physiological.

Houellebecq's physical appearance as relayed in the press suggests that he fully inhabits the word he describes. He looks like a man who has crawled out of a giant ashtray after a prolonged alcoholic binge in clothes that have not been washed for weeks. This does not mean, however, that he approves of the world he inhabits: it is simply that he can conceive of no other, at least for Western man, and if anyone thinks otherwise he is deceiving himself. Grunge is reality; everything else is veneer.

The very success of the Enlightenment project is the root of its failure. Having eliminated myth and magic from human life, it has crushed belief even in itself out of society. This is suggested with characteristic economy by Houellebecq when his protagonist takes a trip, arbitrarily and without clear purpose, to a village called Martel, named after Charles Martel, the victor of the Battle of Poitiers in 732 A.D. that halted the advance of Islam. He, the protagonist of *Soumission*, reflects that in these parts "Cro-Magnon man [once] hunted the mammoth and the reindeer; nowadays they have the choice between an Auchan and a Leclerc [two large supermarket chains], both situated in Souillac." Bravery and excitement have given way to comfort and convenience; degeneration is the inevitable and unavoidable result.

It is not to the point that the Western world, as Houellebecq characterizes it, is in fact much more complex, much less dispiriting, than he allows, that technical advance continues, for example, or that not everyone leads the semi-Hobbesian life (nasty, brutish, solitary, and long) that he describes. This would be to take *Brave New World* and *Nineteen Eighty-Four* as weather forecasts rather than as warnings of tendencies: warnings that, by alerting people to the dangers to which they advert, might help to avert catastrophe. Houellebecq is a visionary rather than an empirical sociological researcher; if he insists on living the life that his books tells us is, or might be, our future, one can only surmise that it is because of psychological peculiarities of his own.

The plot of *Soumission* is simple, but clever and plausible (which does not, of course, mean that, being set in the future, it is a prediction). Having won another mandate of five years in 2017, François Hollande presides over further catastrophic economic and social decline. In the elections of 2022, a four-cornered fight among the Socialist Party, the Movement for a Popular Union (Sarkozy's party), the National Front, and the Muslim Fraternity (a new Islamic political formation imagined by the author, supposedly moderate, led by Mohammed Ben Abbes, a graduate of one of France's elite *grandes écoles* and the son of Algerian immigrants), results in the national Front coming first and the Muslim Fraternity second. In the run-off election, the latter wins easily, however, with both the socialists and the Popular Union supporting it rather than the National Front and going into coalition with (now) President Ben Abbes.

Meanwhile, the Muslim Fraternity has modeled itself on the Muslim Brotherhood and, confident of demographic developments in France that work to Islam's advantage and with a clear understanding that ultimately culture is more important in determining a society's future than its economy, insists only on controlling the schools and universities.

The protagonist and narrator of *Soumission* is a teacher of French literature in a Parisian University, a specialist in the work of Joris-Karl Huysmans, principally known today for his novel of decadent aestheticism, *À rebours*. This was a clever choice on the part of Houellebecq, for Huysmans returned to Catholicism later in life and became an oblate, his last book being *Les foules de Lourdes* (The Crowds of Lourdes). In other words, Huysmans followed the path that the protagonist, in desperate need to escape his current nihilistic condition, will follow; but Catholicism, in the meantime, having lost its faith and becoming, under Pope Francis, little more than transcendental social work to the hosannas of the right-thinking, there is no living faith in France except Islam for him to convert to. It is Islam, *faute de mieux*.

The subtlety of Houellebecq's book consists of demonstrating that the spiritual need of the protagonist can be made to coincide with his material interest. The universities are closed for a time after the accession of Ben Abbes to power, but re-open sometime thereafter. Teachers such as the protagonist of *Soumission* are offered redundancy on full pension, which he at any rate is happy to take. The alternative is continuing in his post, at a salary three times greater than that before, the difference being paid for by subventions from Saudi Arabia and Qatar—subventions which, incidentally, allow the universities of Paris to escape from their dispiriting grunginess under French state finance to some semblance of the grandeur of the medieval Sorbonne. But the *quid pro quo* for receiving the higher salary and being permitted to teach at the university at all is conversion to Islam.

At first the protagonist accepts early retirement on a full pension; but if his life had been essentially empty before such retirement—the work of teaching literature at university level being absurd, leading either a tiny minority of students to perpetuate the teaching of literature, or a great majority of them to work completely unconnected to their studies—it becomes a complete vacuum thereafter.

The generous conditions of retirement deplete the universities of most teachers of standing, but the Saudi and Qatari paymasters are anxious that "their" universities should retain and, if possible, increase their world prestige and standing (just as the Qatari owners of the most famous French football club, Paris Saint-Germain, want "their" club to be among the most prominent in Europe, to the immense financial advantage of the footballers who play in it, most of whom are actually about as Parisian as Doctor Johnson). Whatever else the protagonist may be, he is at least an outstanding scholar of Huysmans's life and work—because there are not many others. He himself is under no illusions about the significance, intellectual or practical, of his expertise, but the prestige of a university, even for those who, such as the new paymasters or de facto owners of the Parisian universities, never pick up a book, depends upon its reputation for scholarship.

The academic head of the protagonist's university, Professor Rediger, had long been known for his Islamophilia, anti-Zionism, and support for the academic boycott of Israel before the arrival of President Ben Abbes in power. Of Belgian origin and Catholic background, he has converted to Islam, but remains worldly and sophisticated, and lives in a magnificent Parisian house. He wants to attract the protagonist back into the academic fold and invites him to that house, where he serves a really excellent Meursault to go with the Lebanese mezze. The professor is married polygamously, first to an older woman responsible for the smooth running of his household and second to a fifteen-year-old girl who excites him sexually and who is not permitted to reveal herself to another man except fully covered.

The protagonist does not feel able to ask the professor why he still drinks alcohol despite a clear prohibition against doing so by his new religion. To ask such a question would be naive, unworldly, or priggish, and enough of the old Parisian savoir vivre remains under the new dispensation, at least for the moment, for the protagonist not to want to appear naive, unworldly, or priggish, as he would if he asked this most obvious question, the kind that a mere Anglo-Saxon would ask. And the professor's relations with his two wives—perhaps he has two more hiding somewhere— seem to be those of effortless domination, unproblematic in fact. Since the protagonist's relations with women have always been difficult, a year with the same woman being the longest he has ever managed, in large part because sexual equality so often creates power struggles within a couple, unabashed patriarchy such as that promoted by Islam would be a solution to his loneliness. The Islam of the professor being a state of happy hypocrisy, there seem to be no disadvantages to it.

The professor has written a short book of 128 pages, including calligraphic illustrations, of Muslim apologetics, *Dix questions sur Islam* (Ten Questions on Islam), which has sold three million copies, and which, in best Jesuitical fashion, he hands the protagonist as he is leaving his house. The protagonist finds the book convincing and duly converts before twelve witnesses in the Great Mosque in Paris. There is a cocktail party afterwards to celebrate his conversion. The latter is of great value to him: soon afterwards he returns to giving his university courses, with their "pretty, veiled, timid female students." He is now in seventh heaven: "Each of these girls, however pretty they might be, felt happy and proud to be chosen by me, and felt honored to share my bed. They deserved to be loved; and, for my part, I came to love them." The protagonist has reached a sublunary Islamic heaven: in effect limitless economic ease and any number of virgins at his disposal. There the book ends.

It is seldom that liberty of any kind is lost all at once," wrote Hume. "Slavery has so frightful an aspect to men accustomed to freedom that it must steal in upon them by degrees and must disguise itself in a thousand shapes in order to be received." This book is, or could be considered, an illustration of Hume's insight. The author does not feel it necessary to point out that the protagonist, having converted, will not be free to apostatize should he subsequently decide that he has made a mistake; Islam is like a vein, it has an built-in mechanism of preventing backflow, so that conversions flow in one direction only. Free enquiry on many subjects will henceforth be denied him, and eventually even the subject of his scholarship is likely to be prohibited, though perhaps not straightaway.

This novel is far from a crude anti-Islamic polemic, however, as many might have supposed it to be from its pre-publication publicity (Houellebecq has expressed himself very unfavorably on Islam elsewhere). It is rather a meditation, admittedly using all the author's habitual tropes which fortunately, or perhaps unfortunately, are susceptible to an infinite number of bitterly amusing variations, on the state of Western civilization and what makes that civilization vulnerable to attack from so intellectually nugatory a force as Islamism which, by all reasonable standards, has nothing of any value whatever to say to the inhabitants of the 21st Century. In other words, it is an implicit invitation to us to look inwards, to think of what is wrong with us rather than with them. Whether we or they will read it like this, I rather doubt. As to a solution, it is hardly the place of a novel to supply it. But whatever it might be, Islam is certainly not it.

Political apologies for the past actions: meaningless and useless

Guilt, it used to be said, was an expression of conscience, but we moderns have found a way of divorcing the one from the other. The avowal of guilt now has nothing to do with conscience, and floats free of anything the person claiming guilt may himself have done or omitted to do.

There was an excellent and typical example of this dissociation in a recent edition of the French newspaper, *Libération*. It was an article by Louis Michel, a Belgian minister and member of the European parliament, entitled "When Belgium apologised to the Rwandan people". The occasion of the article was the first visit of the Rwandan president, Paul Kagame, to France which, you may remember, was accused of having supported the genocidal Hutu government up to the last possible moment. Official relations between Rwanda and France have improved because, it seems, both now need each other.

The author begins in an unctuously self-congratulatory way:

> On the occasion of the official visit of the Rwandan President, Paul Kagame, to France, which seals the normalisation of relations between two friends of Belgium, in which I cannot but rejoice, let me be allowed to testify to the manner in which my country has turned the page in our past relations with Rwanda, in order to look to the future.

In all that follows, there is not a single identifiable individual who is alleged to have done anything wrong, certainly not the author himself.

The nearest he comes to blaming anyone is the following:

> We are convinced that at the time of the genocide the Belgian authorities could, and should, have acted differently in order to have prevented it.

What the Belgians could and should have done is not specified for the readers of the newspaper, who can hardly be expected to know, nor is the identity of the people who should have done it specified. Then follows a passage equally remarkable for its moral grandiosity and its racist condescension:

> It follows that it is right that Belgium should agree to assume a moral responsibility for the Rwandan drama. Not to recognise or to deny the failure of our authorities leaves the Rwandans to bear the burden of this trauma alone.

Let us remind ourselves briefly what happened. About 800,000 people were massacred in about ten weeks in 1994, mainly with machetes. It seems obvious that the overwhelming moral responsibility for this lies with the people who provoked, ordered, organised and performed the massacres, that is to say with those many Rwandans who did any or all of those things.

For foreigners to assume a significant part of the guilt is both to puff themselves up with moral importance and to deny the agency of those who actually were responsible. For M. Michel, then, the Rwandans are still not fully adult, and therefore not fully capable by themselves of committing evil. Belgium, for him, still stands in *loco parentis* for all Rwandans. This demonstrates how deeply entrenched colonial attitudes still are, especially in those who so self-consciously reject them.

Then comes a wonderfully subtle piece of dishonesty:

> Although the political party of the Prime Minister of the day
> [when the apology was made] had not been in power at the
> time of the events, it was fundamental, in the name of the
> continuity of institutions, that we should assume our part of
> the responsibility.

In other words, when we say "we", we don't mean "us", we mean "them, our political opponents". And, of course, nothing is easier – or more gratifying – than to apologise for what your ancestors, enemies or political opponents have done or omitted to do. We get the kudos for having apologised, they get the blame for what we apologise for.

Paragraph after paragraph is stuffed with sentiment that makes greeting-card poetry look Shakespearean in its realism and subtlety. I will quote briefly so as not to provoke nausea:

> To have recognised the mistakes and injustices of the past,
> to have affirmed that we share the responsibility for this
> frightful human waste was, in our view, to open the way to a
> reunification of the heart and minds of all Rwandans.

Can anyone's thoughts and feelings actually correspond to this sentimental drivel? Let us pinch ourselves to remind us that it comes from the pen of a man who holds office and who remains a member of the European political class.

When people indulge in high-flown nonsense, it is legitimate to ask what end such nonsense serves. I have already pointed out that this particular example allows the writer to assume a position of supposedly disinterested moral grandeur while taking a poke at his political opponents. It allows him, as one of the righteous, to enter the Kingdom of Heaven without, however, having to pay an admission fee. And no doubt it allows him to feel a little better about his own peccadilloes, whatever they might be: for what could they possibly be to set against complicity with genocide?

But there is a further advantage. In the very same edition of *Libération*, there is an article about Kagame's Rwanda, in which we read not only of the understandable democratic deficits of the regime (censorship, constant surveillance of the population etc.), but the following remarkable sentence:

> The country, very poor in minerals, has enriched itself with
> war booty brought back from the Democratic Republic of
> Congo and with the massive pillage of cobalt mines.

If I remember correctly, it has been estimated by those who follow such matters that the war in the Congo, from which derive the enriching war booty and pillage of the cobalt mines, has so far cost three or four million lives, that is to say four or five times as many as the Rwandan genocide itself.

It is curious that the newspaper article passes over this sentence without commentary. But it is not at all curious that M. Michel should do so; for if he had noticed it, and its rather deep significance, it would have forced him to think that perhaps Mr Kagame was not quite the hero of a morality play, as a result of which he would actually have to think hard about what attitude, if any, Belgium should now take to the situation in the region. And it is always easier to be moral about what other people have done in the past that to be moral about what one has oneself to do in the present. It is for this reason that political apologies for the past actions of others have become so flourishing a genre.

The Social Affairs Unit, September 14, 2011

Banal memories of fatwa

A review of *Joseph Anton: A Memoir* by Salman Rushdie

Several writers have been sentenced to death and reprieved: Dostoyevsky, for example, Arthur Koestler, and the greatest of all South African writers, Herman Charles Bosman. The first participated at a time of revolution in a circle that read subversive literature, the second was a political conspirator, and the third shot his stepbrother dead in a quarrel. But none lived under the shadow of the executioner for a fraction as long as Salman Rushdie—if the Ayatollah Khomeini's thuggish fatwa can properly be called a death sentence rather than a Mafia-like contract.

Joseph Anton is a memoir of Rushdie's post-fatwa existence. Its title is the false name that he took when he went into police-protected hiding, and consists of the first names of two authors whom Rushdie admires but does not in the least resemble, either in style or quality, Conrad and Chekhov.

The Rushdie affair, as it became known, was an important turning point in world history. In many countries, Islamism rushed in to fill the ideological vacuum left by a decomposing and self-evidently failed Marxism (mankind is always on a search for a theory of everything, when by "everything" is meant its discontents). The Ayatollah's fatwa was one of the first gauntlets thrown down to the western liberal democracies; to change the metaphor rather drastically, it tested the waters, whether that was its original intention or not.

Apart from the somewhat reluctant British decision to protect Rushdie at all costs, the West responded in a vacillating way. Which was more important to us: our freedom or our trade? Sometimes the one, sometimes the other. Were we prepared to stand up for our right to free speech, or did we prefer to censor ourselves for the sake of not offending a minority, or at any rate the rabble-rousing leaders of a minority, in our midst? Sometimes the one, sometimes the other. And the intellectual class, that one might have hoped would see at once what was at stake, was deeply divided, with prominent members in effect siding with the Ayatollah. Rushdie quite rightly quotes Hugh Trevor-Roper's remark to the effect that he would not mind if someone would "waylay [Rushdie] in a dark street and improve his manners," because "society would benefit and literature would not suffer." In the circumstances, it was an odious thing to have said, combining as it does sniggering schoolboy frivolity with a serious error of historical judgment.

Rushdie's personality and character, alas, became a confounding factor in the controversy. It was, of course, completely irrelevant to the matter at issue; I am not myself a believer that politics can or should be nothing but the application of first principles by a process of syllogistic reasoning, but if ever there were a case where a principle should have been decisive, this was it. Unfortunately, the fact that Rushdie was widely disliked, was thought to be arrogant and spoilt, a privileged member of an elite posing as a spokesman for the downtrodden of whom he knew nothing and with whom he would have disdained all contact, got in the way of clear thinking. To this day, discussions of the affair quickly degenerate into an assessment of his character. Only a month ago I participated in a serious discussion of the affair in which someone piped up that if only Rushdie had been more *simpático*, some compromise could have been found.

This seems to me an example of the tendency in modern life to make personal what should be abstract, a tendency that oddly enough coexists with an opposite tendency to make abstract what is personal. In British courts, for example, the victim impact statement has become part of the proceedings in a murder trial (the victim, of course, being the spouse, lover, parent, sibling or best friend of the deceased, rather than the deceased himself). The point about murder, however, is that it is murder, and not that—what F. Tennyson Jesse called—the murderee had lovely eyelashes, a captivating smile, a good sense of humor, will be much missed, etc. Indeed, the whole purpose of the law is to remove such emotionalism from judgment: for it is not only revenge that, as Francis Bacon said, ought to be weeded out as a kind of wild justice. There are other kinds of emotional responses that need to be weeded out.

The judgment of a memoir such as Rushdie's, however, cannot be the same as the judgment of his case. A memoir is not good because the memoirist as a man deserves, as a matter of fundamental principle, our support and protection; and unfortunately Rushdie's book is long and he is not a good writer. On the contrary, he is self-indulgent and much of his account is deeply (or perhaps I should say shallowly) banal, consisting of accounts of takeaway meals or brief and semi-clandestine meetings with well-known persons or full-blown celebrities, of whose fame he seems to be in awe. What he says about these meetings does not rise even to the interest of the gossip column.

He uses the curious literary device throughout of referring to himself in the third person, as "he" rather than "I." Occasionally this is confusing, so that sometimes one is for a moment unsure whether "he" is Rushdie or his interlocutor; but it has a certain psychological advantage for Rushdie, allowing him, for example, to distance himself somewhat from his cad-like behavior towards his third wife and mother of his second son. Here he describes the beginning of his immature affair with the woman who was to become his fourth, but not final, wife:

> He was a married man. His wife and their two-year-old child were waiting for him at home, and if things had been different there he would have grasped the obvious truth that an apparition who seemed to embody everything he hoped for in his future, a Lady Liberty of flesh and blood, had to be a mirage, and that to plunge towards her as if she were real was to court disaster for himself, inflict unconscionable pain upon his wife, and place an unfair burden on the Illusion herself.

It is clear that this passage (about things of doubtful public interest or importance, unless the writer believes that all that pertains to him is *ipso facto* of public interest or importance) would have been much more painful to write, and genuinely confessional, if it had been in the first person. As for the things that would have been different if things had been different, one is reminded of Edmund's great speech:

> This is the excellent foppery of the world, that, when we are sick in fortune (often the surfeit of our own behavior), we make guilty of our disasters the sun, the moon, and the stars: as if we were villains by necessity; fools by heavenly compulsion; knaves, thieves, and treachers, by spherical predominance; drunkards, liars, and adulterers, by an enforced obedience of planetary influence; and all that we are evil in, by a divine thrusting on: An admirable evasion of whore-master man, to lay his goatish disposition to the charge of a star!

In this connection, it worth quoting from the preface to Koestler's account of his time under sentence of death. "The main difficulty," he said, "was the temptation to cut a good figure." This is a thought whose concision and precision is quite beyond Rushdie's powers; and when Rushdie feels that he cannot cut a good figure, as when he recounts his issuance of a grovellingly insincere recantation of his supposed apostasy, he cannot bring himself (as would be natural) actually to quote it. What Rushdie does not realize is that no one with any imagination would blame him for it; here truly was an instance where, if things had been different, things would not only have been different but very different. Anyone can understand how a man under a real threat of death might recant ignominiously in the hope of living longer. As Koestler says, "To die—even in the service of an impersonal cause—is always a personal affair": another of his many thoughts that is worth more than the whole of Rushdie's 656 pages.

To judge by his writing, Rushdie thinks in clichés. I opened the book at random and found the following:

> He was deliberately trying to up the ante, and so far the Iranians were hanging tough and refusing to fold. But there was only one way to go now.

Perhaps a desperate need to escape a mind full of clichés explains the exaggerated imagery of much of his writing, the magic realism with both the magic and the realism removed (in contrast to that of his most ill-chosen, because inimitable, model, Gabriel García Márquez). With him, unlikelihood serves for imagination and emphasis for force. Here he imagines how he might one day write about his experiences:

If he ever wrote a book about these years, how would he do it? . . . He began to think of a project provisionally called "Inferno" in which he could try to turn his story into something other than simple autobiography. A hallucinatory portrait of a man whose picture of the world had been broken. . . . He had lived in that picture and understood why it was the way it was, and how to find his way around inside it. Then like a great hammer swinging the fatwa smashed the picture and left him in an absurd formless amoral universe in which danger was everywhere and sense was not to be found. The man in his story tried desperately to hold his world picture together but the pieces of it came away in his hand like mirror shards and cut his hands until they bled. In his demented state, in this dark wood, the man with the bleeding hands who was a version of himself made his way towards the daylight, through the inferno, in which he passed through the numberless circles of hell, the private and public hells, into the secret worlds of terror, and towards the great, forbidden thoughts.

This is rank bad writing, that of an hysterical adolescent; compare it with the opening lines of Koestler's *Dialogue with Death*:

> For the last six weeks there had been a lull in the fighting. The winter was cold; the wind from the Guadarrama whipped Madrid; the Moors in their trenches caught pneumonia and spat blood.

Comment is redundant.

Sometimes Rushdie, having quoted Hemingway on the art of good writing, and having tired of the effort to be emphatic or imaginative, descends into Hemingwayese:

> He flew back to London and had his eyelids adjusted until they looked normal, and celebrated Milan's second birthday and Zafar's twentieth and then he was fifty-two.

The comma between normal and and would no doubt have met with Ernest's disapproval.

The only passages in the book that I found at all interesting or moving were those concerning his parents. His father was a member of India's anglicized elite, who descended into alcoholism; his mother, with whom his father had a relationship of hostile dependence, had been married before to a man whom she passionately loved but who was unable to give her children. In those days, this was good grounds for divorce; he never remarried, and in the sixteen years of her widowhood, she could have taken up with him (she never ceased to love him) but did not. Here truly was a Chekhovian situation, altogether more interesting than Rushdie's own rather sordid squabbles which he recounts in their banal detail.

Most of Joseph Anton is decidedly dull, neither revelatory of the experience or psychology of clandestinity nor illuminating about the political aspects of the affair. Koestler's *Dialogue with Death* and Herman Charles Bosman's *Cold Stone Jug* are incomparably better (and shorter). Rushdie repeatedly says in the book that he is a writer and appears to think that he is a great one, since he has been told so many times by people who ought to know. It is not surprising, then, that he treats with contumely reports that many of his readers cannot get through his novels, finding them badly written, boring, incomprehensible, etc. For him this is an urban legend, but a straw poll of my friends suggests that it is very far from being such a myth. No doubt Rushdie would respond that Mr. and Mrs. Average find Dostoyevsky hard to get through, but my friends are, from the point of view of literary knowledge and appreciation, Mr. and Mrs. Well-Above-Average.

As it happens I was also reading Jan Morris's book about Trieste while I was reading Joseph Anton. Towards the end of Morris's book, she writes:

> A great city [such as Trieste] that has lost its purpose is like a specialist in retirement. He potters around the house. He tinkers with this hobby or that. He reads a little, watches television for half an hour, does a bit of gardening, determines once more that he really will read *Midnight's Children*.

The New Criterion, May 2016

Pondering the Immigration Imponderables

The relationship between personal experience and public policy is not at all straightforward, and of no aspect of public policy is this more true than that of illegal immigration. In Europe, the question is daily put before us by newspapers, magazines, blogs, radio, and television, with dramatic pictures of desperate illegal immigrants trying to reach our shores across the Mediterranean, many of them drowning en route. Even without such media coverage, however, the change in the ethnic and cultural origins of the inhabitants of our towns and cities is so obvious that no one could possibly miss it. Some glory in the change, some detest it; it is difficult to be neutral, or even merely objective, about it.

Although Europe is mired, for the moment, in economic stagnation (how long for is a matter of speculation), it is vastly rich, prosperous and stable compared to the countries from which the immigrants generally come. Even Greece seems a promised land to them, though mainly as a jumping-off point from which to reach a richer country yet.

On the subject of illegal immigrants, and the wider one of the change in the ethic and cultural composition of our societies, I confess that my thoughts and feelings are inconsistent and contradictory. I am myself the son of a refugee, and in my work as a doctor in a hospital in an area that came to be inhabited by, if not exactly to welcome, many refugees and illegal immigrants I came to almost always to sympathize with, and often to admire, them as individuals.

The difference between political refugees and economic migrants did not seem to me as important as it seemed to our authorities, for even the economic migrants were fleeing conditions that were unimaginably hard. The people I came to know were brave and enterprising, and had no desire to sponge on the state, but rather to work and improve their lives. Although they had no legal right to anything but emergency medical care, I ended up being primary care physician to them because they had no one else to turn to.

Perhaps it helped that I had been to most of the countries from which they came: the Congo, Iran, Somalia, and so forth. For a native Briton to speak to them who knew even a little of their country must have come as some slight relief to them in a sea of strangeness, incomprehension, hostility, or indifference. I too enjoyed talking to them. It allowed me to feel benevolent at no great cost to myself.

It does seem to be the case that we need people to come to us from impoverished lands, and this is so despite the fact that we have a substantial fund of unemployed people. Why this should be I leave to labour economists to decide; I suspect it has something to do with the rent-seeking behavior of a very large percentage of our population (including me). But let me just describe the case of my mother-in-law living in Paris, now so infirm that she needs the assistance of three people working in shifts to allow her to remain at home.

These three are women who come from Cabo Verde, Mauritius, and Haiti. Whether they were ever illegal immigrants I do not know; but they are now legal residents of France and are paid in regular fashion, taxed normally and with all the rights of those who work in the official economy.

All three of them do far more for my mother-in-law than they are paid to do, not because of any attempt on our part to exploit them, but because they are extremely good people, whose warmth, kindness, humanity and mannerliness were obvious on first acquaintance. Indeed, these qualities induce a slight feeling of shame in belonging to a culture in which these qualities should seem exceptional rather than normal. It is we, not they, who are so often crude.

It so happened that when I first met the Haitian lady I had just been to an exhibition of Haitian art whose catalogue I showed her; moreover, my wife and I had been to Haiti (in my case more than once) and so were able to talk to her of Haitian history and literature. We discovered what is too easily overlooked in immigrants from poor countries, namely that she was a refined and educated person, though one who felt no shame in her work as caregiver to an old lady. Having made our acquaintance, she immediately brought us a present of a bottle of Haitian rum which, by the way, is by far the best that I know; its cost represented two and a half hours of her labor. She delights to cook Haitian dishes for us, doing this for the pleasure that our thanks give her. She is a woman who laughs at hardship, whose generosity of spirit is obvious.

The other two caregivers have different virtues, but are just as virtuous. And without the help of these women, we should either have to put my mother-in-law in a home or look after her ourselves, disrupting—not to say dominating—our lives entirely.

Having conveyed my personal experience, I musn't shy from the question: is one's personal experience sufficient to fashion a proper attitude or policy towards immigration, legal or illegal? I am not so unprejudiced a person that I view with delight the disappearance of the culture in which I grew up, which is being absorbed into a kind of cultural minestrone of no particular savour. Nor do I think that to know another culture is simply a matter of patronizing a restaurant of its cuisine from time to time. It is, rather, the work of years if not of a lifetime. Consider that multiculturalism therefore condemns us to be strangers to one another; and, while all cultures have their charms, they may not all be compatible in their conceptions.

The economic effects of mass immigration into European countries are disputed. Some claim that it leads to economic growth, but this is not the answer to the real economic question, which is whether it leads to age-adjusted per capita economic growth.

Even if this question could be answered affirmatively and beyond all doubt or debate, there would still remain the question of whether, for other reasons, it would be undesirable. The fact is that most people who support mass immigration are personally less keen on taking the social consequences of it. In France, for example, someone not long ago contacted more than 40 media personalities who publicly supported immigration and asked them whether they could assist personally with lodging an immigrant. Though each was rich, none said he could do so for more than a day or two, each finding a good excuse for his inability.

In summary, then:

I sympathize personally with the immigrants;

I like the majority of those whom I have met;

I recognize that, along with many others, I benefit from their presence, though I do not know precisely what the size of that presence ought to be;

I do not know what their overall economic effect is;

I do not want to see my society changed irreversibly by their uncontrolled influx.

What, then, is the right policy?

Library of Law and Liberty, 25 June, 2015

Rich Man, Poor Man:
No Insults Allowed

A well-known religious figure is reported to have said: "For ye have the poor with you always." This is even more the case if economic inequality persists (as the history of the world suggests it might) and poverty is defined in relative terms. The same well-known figure added, however, that "whensoever ye will, ye may do them good."

The question, of course, becomes what constitutes good in this context.

A new way of doing the poor good has been proposed in France: namely, a legal prohibition of pejorative remarks about them. It's an idea that a British journalist, writing in the *Guardian*, found worthy of adoption in her own country. We may not be able to reduce poverty (howsoever defined), but at least we can boost the self-esteem of the poor and stop them feeling bad about themselves. Such, at any rate, is the theory.

Poverty, said Doctor Johnson, is an insufficiency of necessities, but this definition is far less categorical than might at first appear since what is considered a necessity tends to expand with general wealth and technical advance. I suspect that, given the choice between wholesome food and a mobile telephone, many people in the modern world would choose the telephone. No matter how much infant mortality declines or life expectancy increases, no matter what the rising tide of consumption, then, the poor we shall continue to have with us.

In a world that is supposedly meritocratic, in which the possibility of social mobility is believed to be the norm, morally if not empirically, the poor—the relatively poor, that is—have two choices, neither of them very attractive: to consider themselves failures or, as a way of avoiding doing so, to resent the difference between the world as it is supposed to be and the world as (they believe) it is. And since belief is often a determining feature of reality, the world does indeed come to resemble the one of their imagining. Even where there is opportunity, or at least no formal obstacle to advancement, they do not register this, for the manacles forged by their minds are gratifying. By which I mean being a victim of injustice has more appeal than being a failure.

No one, as far as I know, has yet advanced the idea that the rich should be protected from derogation. The same newspaper whose columnist thought it would be a good idea to censor unpleasant or insulting comments about the poor regularly publishes cartoons that, with all the subtlety of *Der Stürmer*, use iconography little changed from that of a century ago. Vilifying the rich is taken by the newspaper as the sign of a generous heart, and furthermore, one which costs nothing.

The rich are, of course, a small minority. We are constantly reminded of the division of the population into the 99 percent and the 1 percent—references to which always leave me worrying neurotically about which category I belong in, my desire to be among the economically successful conflicting with a desire to be inconspicuous and ordinary. In any case it is always carelessly supposed that the members of this small group can look after themselves and require no anti-discriminatory assistance from lawmakers. The feelings of the rich do not have to be spared because 1) they have other compensations and 2) they can defend themselves.

Let us disregard the economic status of the rich and just consider the indisputable history of the 20th Century. If communism counts as a form of economic egalitarianism and therefore as a movement to destroy or abolish the rich as a class, ideological antagonism toward the rich may be said to have been responsible for scores of millions of deaths. This is not altogether surprising, for if poverty is relative, so is wealth: As countries decline in wealth, so a poorer and poorer man will come to be regarded as wealthy. In Russia a kulak was often defined as a man who owned a horse, cow, or pig, and was therefore considered as an exploiter—of his fellow man, not of the horse, cow, or pig— and rightly to be eliminated. But no matter how much elimination you go in for, ye have the rich with you always.

Few emotions are as easy to stir but as difficult to control as envy and hatred of the rich. What Freud called the narcissism of small differences means that increased equality does not necessarily assuage or lessen such hatred, for there is no end to the pettiness of humankind. How much envy and jealousy are provoked by trifling differences in status?

If it were right, then, to censor the expression of dangerous or unpleasant sentiments, it would be right above all to censor expressions of economic egalitarianism, a doctrine that proved so dangerously inflammatory only a few decades ago and that we have no reason to believe could not have the same terrible effects again. Under such a law, anyone who argued that the rich *ipso facto* exploited the poor would be subject to prosecution for a form of so-called hate speech that has abundantly demonstrated its potential for provoking violence.

This proposal, incidentally, could be justified irrespective of the actual conduct of the rich. Personally I have not found the rich to be much better (or worse) than the poor, though it is surely easy enough to understand that if poverty is often an extenuation of bad behavior, wealth is sometimes an aggravating circumstance. But what we are concerned with here is not the actual conduct of the rich, but the effects—and they have been historically disastrous—of provoking hatred of them.

I hope it is needless to say that I do not really think people who shout "Rich bastard!" (odd how the connotation of the word bastard has survived social acceptance of bastardy itself), or even Nobel prize-winning economists such as Paul Krugman, should be hauled away and prosecuted. For the term "hate-speech" is itself hateful—a provocation of the very emotion that those who make use of it claim to hate.

Preserving them from insult will do them no more good, at least in a secularized world, than telling them they are the beloved of God.

Library of Law and Liberty, 26 August 2015

Europe's Bloodless Universalism

By now the story of Omar Ismail Mostefai, the first of the perpetrators of the Paris attacks to be named, is depressingly familiar. One could almost have written his biography before knowing anything about him. A petty criminal of Algerian parentage from what all the world now calls the banlieue, he was sustained largely by the social security system, an erstwhile fan of rap music, and a votary of what might be called the continuation of criminality by other means, which is to say Islamism and the grandiose purpose in life that it gives to its adherents. For feeble minds, the extremity of the consequences for self and others serves as some kind of guarantee that their cause is just.

Nor was the connection to Molenbeek, a neighborhood in Brussels where at least three of the terrorists lived, much of a surprise to anyone. Brussels—the "capital of Europe," be it remembered—is slightly more than a quarter Muslim, and a much higher percentage of Molenbeek's residents are Muslims of North African background. When a few years ago I was shown around the place, my acquaintances told me it was virtually extraterritorial as far as the Belgian state was concerned—apart from the collection of social security, of course.

All the women wore headscarves, and the young men dressed like fans of American rap music. The police rarely entered and were far more concerned not to offend Muslim sensibilities—for example, by not being seen to eat during Ramadan—than to find or capture the miscreants who made the area so dangerously crime-ridden. Businesses there (so my guides told me) paid no taxes but were not investigated for evasion by the tax authorities: it was the tax authorities who did the evading.

Everyone knew Islamist preaching and plotting were rife in Molenbeek, but nothing was done to stop it, in order to keep the tense and fragile peace going as long as possible. Sympathy for terrorism was the norm—or, it would be more correct to say, that no one dared publicly voice opposition to it.

If my informants were right, this was the perfect place for psychopaths with an illusion of purpose to flourish and make plans undisturbed by the authorities, while being supported by the welfare state. Events since have demonstrated that they did not exaggerate (as, to my regret, I rather suspected at the time that they did, for alarm is so often disproportionate to the reality that gives rise to it). Recall that the terrorists who were disarmed on the train from Amsterdam to Paris in August came from Molenbeek, as did the man who killed four people at the Jewish Museum in Brussels in 2014. More volunteers to fight for ISIS have come from Molenbeek than anywhere else in Europe.

The Belgian Prime Minister, Charles Michel, has now virtually admitted that the area was extraterritorial to Belgium, and out of all control. The time had come "to focus more on repression," he said. But whether the determination or sufficient political unity necessary to carry it out will last is doubtful. Repression requires discrimination; we live in a regime in which murderers may come and go, but social security goes on forever.

Do we have the stomach to tar many people with the same brush? That we now know that terrorists among the Syrian refugees have entered Europe, which was precisely the objection of those opposed to accepting them (who were vilified by immigration-liberals for their moral obtuseness or nastiness, and have been proven right, which is even more unforgivable), now raises the disturbing question: How many innocent people should Europe accept for one suicide bomber?

A striking thing about the immigration debate before the massacres of November 13 was the almost complete absence of references, at least by the "respectable" politicians, to the national interest of the various countries. The debate was couched in Kantian moral terms. Sweden, for example, which has no imperative to take refugees other than moral grandiosity and its desire to feel itself virtuous, has had a hard enough time integrating the immigrants it has already taken; their entry has made that country one with nearly the highest crime rate in Western Europe. Current family re-unification laws in Europe mean that the numbers any country agrees to take will soon be expanded.

There is a real moral dilemma, of course. Recently in Bodrum, on the Aegean coast of Turkey, I was approached by a family of four Syrian refugees begging for alms. The father of the family showed me his Syrian passport (precisely of the kind so easily forged by the terrorists), but all I could see was his wife and two small children who were obviously bereft of support and who would obviously suffer without charity. That day, 22 refugees were reported drowned as they tried to reach Turkey by boat, an occurrence so regular that it was not reported in the Western press. No one undertakes such a journey lightly: only safety or an egocentric thirst for "martyrdom" could impel him.

Europe has nothing equivalent to national interest, and if it did, it would have no way of acting on it. A kind of bloodless universalism has rushed in to fill the vacuum, whose consequences are now visible to all. The first thing President Hollande tried to do after the attacks was close the borders; he now talks (understandably, of course) of national security. He talks also of defeating ISIS militarily, but France, along with all of the other European countries, has run down its armed forces in the name of the social security that paid for at least some of the terrorists.

Just because Europe's weakness is clear doesn't mean that our heads are clear. Three days after the attacks, the most influential newspaper in Britain (and in certain ways the best), the liberal-left *Guardian*, ran 40 small photos of some the victims, with the headline, "Killed in the Pitiless Name of Terrorism."

They were not killed in the pitiless name of terrorism, of course. They were killed in the pitiless name of Islam—not the only possible interpretation of Islam, no doubt, but still in its name. In the cowardice of this headline was the encapsulated all the weakness of Europe, a real encouragement to the terrorists.

Library of Law and Liberty, 19 November 2015

Playing with Fire

One of the greatest plays of the 20th Century, at least of those known to me, is Max Frisch's *The Fire Raisers* (1953). Written in the aftermath of the Second World War as an attempt to explain (and to warn) how a patent evil like Nazism can triumph in a civilized society, this play does what only great literature can do: suggest the universal while using the particular.

Its protagonist, Biedermann, is a comfortable bourgeois living in a town that is beset by several mysterious acts of arson. He is visited at home by Schmitz, a hawker, who half-persuades, half-intimidates his way into an invitation to lodge in Biedermann's attic, and who soon brings a second hawker, Eisenring, to stay in the house.

Gradually it becomes clear that Schmitz and Eisenring are the ones setting the fires in the town, but Biedermann refuses to acknowledge it. His blindness arises from moral and physical cowardice, and from wishful thinking—the hope that what he sees does not really mean what it obviously means. Schmitz and Eisenring bring barrels of gasoline into the house and Biedermann, pusillanimous to the last, helps them make the fuses and gives them the matches with which they burn his house down.

Now most of us have worked for organizations or institutions that have acceded to changes we think immoral or deleterious and which, if extended in the same direction, could lead to disaster. At what point do we resist? We do not have the luxury of knowing how it all turns out. We don't want to be Biedermann; on the other hand, we can't resist to the last ditch every change with which we disagree. There is no one so tiresome or ineffectual as the permanent, uncompromising oppositionist who sees in every slight phenomenon of which he disapproves the slippery slope to human damnation. Not every slippery slope is slid down; and in any case, experience shows us, or should show us, our judgment is fallible.

Nevertheless, I could not help but think of Biedermann recently as I read an account in *Le Monde*, the French newspaper of record, of the Greece versus Turkey soccer match held in Istanbul in the presence of the two countries' prime ministers. The event was supposed to symbolize political reconciliation between these historically antagonistic countries.

Personally, I have never been fully convinced that international sport serves to improve relations between nations. Such gestures strike me as often bordering on emotional kitsch. Not only that, they can have the reverse effect: that of bringing out the crudest nationalist feelings in crowds.

What happened on this occasion was even worse than that. When a minute's silence was called for before the match as a mark of respect or mourning for the victims of the November 13 terrorist attacks in Paris, it provoked a counter-demonstration. The crowd—what proportion of it will never be known—began to whistle and to chant *Allahu akbar*, "God is great."

The most obvious interpretation of this disgusting episode is that a considerable public feeling exists in Turkey (whose extent is necessarily unknown) that rejoices in the mass murder of "infidels."

But the *Le Monde* reporter struggled, or rather squirmed, to avoid this most obvious interpretation. Biedermann himself could not have done better.

This is what the article said, inter alia:

> The [Turkish] prime minister, Davutoglu, did not react. 'The martyrs are eternal, the country is indivisible!' chanted the supporters.
>
> We don't know if this hostility was directed at the victims of the attacks of November 13, or at the Greek prime minister, or both.
>
> The slogan in question is usually chanted by Turkish patriots whenever a Turkish soldier (called 'martyr') is killed by rebel Kurds of the PKK [the Kurdish Workers' Party].
>
> With the recrudescence of hostilities between the PKK and the Turkish Army, this kind of slogan has returned to the streets and stadiums with a vengeance. On 13 October, at a qualifying match for the European Cup in Konya, a conservative city in central Anatolia, shouts of 'Allahu akbar' rang out from the stands to break the minute's silence observed to commemorate the 102 victims (all militants of the left-wing pro-Kurdish party) of the double suicide bombing in Ankara three days earlier. The combination of 'Allahu akbar' and 'The country is indivisible' signals the return to the ideology of the ultra- nationalists in vogue in the 1970s . . .

But it is perfectly obvious that the attacks in Paris had nothing whatever to do with Turkish nationalism (no suspect was Turkish, and Turkish nationals were more likely to be victims of the attacks than perpetrators of them), nor were the victims targeted because they were pro-Kurdish. If anything, the perpetrators would have been anti-Turkish nationalism, in so far as such nationalism is competitive with Islamic fundamentalism.

The chant of 'Allahu akbar' during the minute's silence before the soccer match expressed a religious, not a nationalistic, sentiment. This is so perfectly obvious that one wonders why the author of the article assiduously avoided saying it.

The parallel with Frisch's hapless protagonist is not exact, of course, because two of the interlopers he let in his house, whose activities he was at such dishonest pains to deny, were fire-raisers. We have no means of knowing what percentage of Muslims in France and the rest of Europe abominate, approve, or support what was done in Paris. But Biedermann's state of denial of and that of the *Le Monde* reporter are eerily similar, and similarly dangerous. We should not allow such evasion—a mere 13 days after the bombings!—to go unremarked.

Library of Law and Liberty, 27 November 2015

Pope Francis Should Seek Clarity on Moral Responsibility

One of the consequences of living in an information age is that we are made instantly, and constantly, aware of the disasters around the world, both natural and man-made, and of the enormous suffering that they cause. There are no more far-away lands of which to know nothing, to quote Neville Chamberlain, a man whom nobody would describe as wicked but yet who is the most despised of British Prime Ministers. We are all citizens of the world now.

Knowledge of suffering seems to place upon us an obligation of compassion that is greater than we can possibly bear. We respond in one of two ways: to claim a level of feeling that is greater than we actually can or do feel, in which case we become humbugs; or we harden our hearts and become like Pharaoh. The compassion center in our brain, if such exists (and some neuroscientists claimed to have found the empathy center), is overwhelmed and worn out. A visitor to Mussolini once emerged from his visit exclaiming 'Too many spats! Too many spats!'; our compassion center, in like fashion, cries 'Too many famines! Too many civil wars!' And so we retire to cultivate our garden.

Pope Francis chose Lampedusa recently as his first place to visit outside Rome after his election to the papacy. Lampedusa is an Italian island of 8 square miles with a permanent population of 6000, which so far this year has received 7800 migrants trying to reach Europe across the Mediterranean from sub-Saharan and North Africa, that is to say more than 1000 a month. When the Pope officiated at mass on the island's sports field, there were 10,000 in the congregation, two thirds more than the permanent population, suggesting that the migrants stay a few months at least on Lampedusa. How far the 4000 non-inhabitants of Lampedusa (many of them presumably non-Catholics) attended the mass for religious reasons, and how many for political advantage, may be guessed at but not known.

In effect the island has been transformed into a refugee camp, not necessarily with the approval or agreement of the original inhabitants. This was a *fait accompli* imposed upon them by political, historical and geographical circumstances.

Estimates suggest that about 100 migrants a month for the past twenty years have drowned during their clandestine passage across the Mediterranean towards Europe. This being the case, no one could possibly say that the migrants decided on the journey in a whimsical or light-hearted fashion. The attraction of Europe or the repulsion of their homelands, or both, must be very powerful for so many people to risk so high a chance of so pathetic a death. The Pope said that all his compassion went to the immigrants who had died at sea 'in these boats that, instead of bringing hope of a better life, brought them to death,' and this was right and proper. Surely someone must be lacking in both imagination and feeling not to sorrow for these poor people.

Compassionate fellow-feeling, however, can soon become self-indulgent and lead to spiritual pride. It imparts an inner glow, like a shot of whiskey on a cold day, but like whiskey it can prevent the clear-headedness which we need at least as much as we need warmth of heart. Pascal said that the beginning of morality was to think well; generosity of spirit is not enough.

In his homily, the Pope decried what he called 'the globalization of indifference' to the suffering of which the tragedy of the drowned was a manifestation and a consequence. Our culture of comfort, he said, has made us indifferent to the sufferings of others; we have forgotten how to cry on their behalf. He made reference to the play of Lope de Vega in which a tyrant is killed by the inhabitants of a town called Fuente Ovejuna, no one owning up to the killing and everyone saying that it was Fuente Ovejuna that killed him. The West, said the Pope, was like Fuente Ovejuna, for when asked who was to blame for the deaths of these migrants, it answered, 'Everyone and no one!' He continued, 'Today also this question emerges: who is responsible for the blood of these brothers and sisters? No one! We each reply: it was not I, I wasn't here, it was someone else.'

The Pope also called for 'those who take the socio-economic decisions in anonymity that open the way to tragedies such as these to come out of hiding.'

With all due respect, I think this is very loose thinking indeed of a kind that the last Pope would not have permitted himself. The analogy between the two situations, the murder of the tyrant in Fuente Ovejuna and the death by drowning of thousands of migrants, is weak to the point of non-existence. After all, someone in Fuente Ovejuna did kill the tyrant; no one in the west drowned the migrants. Is the Pope then saying that Europe's refusal to allow in all who want to come is the moral equivalent of actually wielding the knife?

By elevating feeling over thought, by making compassion the

measure of all things, the Pope was able to evade the complexities of the situation, in effect indulging in one of the characteristic vices of our time, moral exhibitionism, which is the espousal of generous sentiment without the pain of having to think of the costs to other people of the implied (but unstated) morally-appropriate policy. This imprecision allowed him to evade the vexed question as to exactly how many of the suffering of Africa, and elsewhere, Europe was supposed to admit and subsidize (and by Europe I mean, of course, the European taxpayer, who might have problems of his own). I was reminded of a discussion in my French family in which one brother-in-law complained to another of the ungenerous attitude of the French state towards immigrants from the Third World. 'Well,' said the other, 'you have room enough. Why don't you take ten Malians?' To this there was no reply except that it was a low blow: though to me it seemed a perfectly reasonable response.

The Pope's use of a term such as 'those who take the socio-economic decisions in anonymity' was strong on connotation but weak on denotation, itself a sign of intellectual evasion. Who, exactly, were 'those' people? Wall Street hedge fund managers, the International Monetary Fund, opponents of free trade, African dictators? Was he saying that the whole world economic system was to blame for the migration across the Mediterranean, that the existence of borders was illegitimate, that Denmark (for example) was rich because Swaziland was poor, that if only Losotho were brought up to the level of Liechtenstein (or, of course, if Liechtenstein were brought down to the level of Lesotho) no one would drown in the Mediterranean? There was something for everyone's conspiracy theory in his words; but whatever else they meant, we were to understand that he was on the side of the little man, not the big, itself a metonym for virtuous sentiment. The only specific group whom the Pope denounced were the traffickers in people, those who arrange passage of the migrants in return for money and who are utterly indifferent to their safety; but this denunciation hardly required moral courage because such people have no defenders.

Warmth of feeling cannot be the sole guide to our responses to the dilemmas that the world constantly puts in our path. There was, for example, a sudden influx of Congolese refugees into the city in which I worked as a doctor. Within a short time a 'community' grew up and in three or four years the Congolese population of the city went from zero to half a per cent of the entire population.

I had quite a few Congolese patients and although the regulations stated that they were to be treated only in emergencies I could hardly refuse them other treatment, and did not. I soon found that I was giving them advice on all sorts of non-medical matters. I liked them as people; often they had suffered terribly; most of them were determined to do their best in their new country. In many ways they were admirable (admirable people often emerge from the most terrible circumstances). It helped our relations that I had once crossed the Congo in the days when it was Zaire and that I knew something of the country's history; to meet someone for whom the Congo was not merely a name, if even that, must have been a relief to them in their isolation.

Despite my sympathy for them (how much better their children behaved than the spoilt brats of the local population!), and the fact that I was willing to break some bureaucratic rules on their behalf, I did not think that the government could very well throw wide open the doors of the country to the Congo and let all who wished come, although there was no reason to suppose that those who would be excluded would be any worse human beings than those who were admitted. There was injustice in this, for some would benefit and others would suffer merely by chance and not by merit or demerit. But to right this injustice would be worse than not to right it: hence the tragedy. The nature of human existence inevitably creates conflict between desiderata.

That is one of the reasons why the kingdom of the Pope's master could not possibly be of this world. And the absence of the tragic sense in the Pope's remarks allowed him to wallow in a pleasing warm bath of sentiment without distraction by complex and unpleasant realities. Perhaps this will earn him applause in the short run; but in the long run he does not serve his flock by such over-simplifications.

Library of Law and Liberty, 22 July 2013

"Thank you, but . . ." ?

My French brother-in-law recently sent me links to videos of two young French Muslims of North African descent inveighing against crimes committed in the name of religion. They were unmistakably angry and sincere. Interestingly, they said it was up to us—that is to say, we, the Muslims of France—to counteract the evil that was besmirching the name and reputation of millions of our coreligionists.

It was a brave performance, because neither of them disguised himself. They probably know many people who—to put it mildly—disagree with them. One could easily imagine them being targeted by extremists. My brother-in-law (whose son was in the Stade de France on the day of the attacks) saw grounds for optimism in these videos.

It is only right and just that we should applaud these two young men whose actions were very courageous (they had families to protect, as well as themselves). It took some brass, as we say in England, to tell their peers that if they didn't like it in France, they should go back to their villages of origin in Morocco or Algeria, and try life there. One of them even compared the French police, no doubt the objects of visceral hatred among many of the young men whom they were addressing, with those of Morocco, and asked them whether they would really prefer to be at the mercy of the Moroccan police.

The videos raised two questions, however, neither of which I could answer fully.

First, let us suppose that the great majority of the Muslims of France agreed with the two men who posted their video disquisitions. Is that majority more significant than the remaining minority? We are, after all, not talking of a peaceful election in which majority opinion triumphs by constitutional means (and even proper elections may result in the establishment of the most terrible dictatorships). Nor is the question a static one: for it involves weighing which tendency, integration or violent rejection, is in the ascendant. And in fact the two can grow simultaneously. Where terrorism is concerned, small numbers can have huge effects. (It is the very purpose of terrorism, come to that.)

The second question concerns the importance of elementary historical truth. The two French Muslims who made the videos were believers. They both said that the perpetrators of the crimes were not really Muslim at all because Islam is a religion of peace. There are, of course, Muslims who choose to interpret it peacefully, and we should be grateful for that; but Islam in fact has a very violent history, even according to its own sources, which may be expected to paint such violence in a favorable light, a fact so obvious as to hardly be worth pointing out. This is so whether or not other religions and doctrines have also had violent histories. Islam (in the words of Edward Gibbon, in the context of the spread of another religion) did not spread merely by the convincing evidence of the doctrine.

Not long ago I had a conversation with a charming, cultivated, and intelligent Egyptian who called himself a liberal believer. I quizzed him on two points that I thought were essential stumbling blocks to Islam's accommodation with the modern world: the first was that of equality before the law, and the second was the freedom openly and publicly to apostatize and argue in opposition to the religion. On these questions he was completely sound (at least from my point of view): he accepted equality before the law and apostasy without legal penalty as being perfectly normal, acceptable, and indeed desirable. Moreover, he was honest enough to admit that his views were held by a small, but he hoped growing, minority of Muslims.

On the question of jihad, he was also sound, but for a historical reason that rather took me aback. Jihad, he said, was no longer justified because there was no legal prohibition anywhere against the preaching of the Muslim message. Jihad had been justified in the past because there had been such prohibition.

It seemed to me an extraordinary reading of history: that the expansion of Islam by force had been only to secure freedom of preaching. Was he claiming that freedom to preach a religious message was a universal right enforceable by violence (in which case, an attack on Saudi Arabia, say, or on Iran, to enforce it would be entirely justified)? Or was he saying that Islam was the only religion that had that right—in which case, we find ourselves in what would have to be called the intellectual antechamber of extremism.

As this was a social occasion, I did not push our discussion further. In any case, it was obvious that my interlocutor was a decent, peace-loving man who would never ordinarily be a terrorist or personally intolerant. So did it really matter if he held an opinion that was mistaken or even absurd? No doubt we all have a tendency to believe six impossible things before breakfast.

If people are peaceful and law-abiding in the belief, say, that Islam is a religion of peace (or indeed in any other belief), should one strive to correct it merely because one holds it to be not merely mistaken, but grossly mistaken? The answer does not seem straightforward.

On the one hand, we do not want so to antagonize such people by dogmatically insisting on what we see as the truth or rubbing their noses in their own errors, lest we drive them into the arms of extremists. On the other hand, not only do we have a basic attachment to historic truth as a value in itself, but there are obvious dangers in accepting historical myth.

So should we just say to the two young men who made the videos, "Thank you," and leave it at that—or should we say, "Thank you, but . . . "?

Library of Law and Liberty, 4 December 2015

Up in Arms About a Coat of Arms

Harvard Law School, in abject surrender to student activists, is about to change its escutcheon because its design was derived from that of Isaac Royall, Jr., who endowed the first chair at the school. Royall's father made the family fortune from slave plantations in the West Indies and Massachusetts, a fortune that was therefore tainted (as Balzac said that all great fortunes are).

Since the escutcheon was adopted only in 1937, it hardly counts as an immemorial symbol of the law school. This is not the destruction of Palmyra, but I doubt that the students who agitated for change were great respecters of antiquity in any case. Like the Salafists, they assess the value of anything and everything according to their own inflexible standards, and demand that monuments and memorials be entirely consistent with their own current moral preoccupations.

How long before they suggest the Palmyran-type destruction of the Washington and Jefferson Memorials in the American capital because both historical figures were slave-owners, and of the Lincoln Memorial into the bargain because, in the 1850s, he said he was not at that moment arguing for the political and social equality of whites and blacks?

On the American website of the British liberal newspaper, the *Guardian*, I found a photo of a Harvard Law student holding a placard in front of him with a beatific look on his face. The placard said:

(let me put this in language HLS will understand:) whether we've failed purposefully, recklessly, or negligently is of no moment. When it comes to the failure to confront structural racism, we must all hold ourselves *strictly liable*. [Emphasis in original]

The psychology of the messenger is, of course, much more interesting than his tedious and tediously-expressed message. It is alarming that a student at an elite, or even hyper-elite, college should think so muddily and write so badly.

Who, exactly, were the "We" to whom the self-satisfied youth addressed himself? Surely he could not have meant the combined students and faculty of the Harvard Law School, for he addressed the faculty with an unmistakable air of condescension, de haut en bas (recurring to language they could understand, as if the faculty were composed of mental defectives). Who, one is tempted to ask, are the teachers at Harvard Law School and who the taught? To adopt the imperative tone that seems to come so naturally to the young moral giants of that institution, we must presume that the "We" refers only to the students.

Vehemence is here a substitute for clarity.

For what and to whom are the students strictly liable? Is this liability legal or merely moral? Is failure to protest henceforth to be made actionable at law? Who will sue whom? Had students at the law school better protest lest they find themselves having to pay damages? If so, to whom, exactly?

Where is Harvard Law School's "structural racism"? If it has an admissions policy that takes applicants' race into consideration, that might be called structurally racist. But it seems to me likely that the institution's structural racism acts in favor of rather than against hitherto disfavored races. (Of course, you can't discriminate positively without discriminating negatively.) More likely the deeply smug student with the placard meant that the law school suffered from some kind of moral dry rot that had entered its fabric, so all-pervasive that it needed (after the student's graduation, of course) to be replaced in its entirety.

What the student really meant is, however, beside the point. He was not intent upon conveying information, much less an argument. He intended to communicate the militant purity of his heart and soul. The world is rotten, he was saying—but I am not. I am pure. If the rottenness continues, it won't be because of me.

Awareness of his own virtue shone from the student's face. He positively glowed with it, virtue for him consisting of the public expression of the correct sentiments. Virtue required no discipline, no sacrifice other than of a little time and energy, instantly rewarded by the exhibition of his own goodness.

The painlessness of virtue as the expression of correct sentiment is, of course, its chief attraction. Who would not wish to achieve goodness merely by means of a few gestures, verbal or otherwise? In that way, you can avoid genuine self-examination altogether. After all, of what importance is your conduct in the little circle around you compared with such enormous wrongs as structural racism?

I have no reason to impugn the young man's private conduct. For all I know, he is an excellent young man except for the shallowness of his prose, and his complacency and self-importance. For many students (if I remember my own past correctly), one's self is one's own ideal.

Then, too, he no doubt felt a youthful impatience with the sheer intractability of the world, and hence a desire that its problems should be solved by purely symbolic means such as a change of escutcheon. This desire partakes of magical thinking: incantations will somehow bend reality in the desired direction.

Still, the moral grandiosity of the student (and those like him) had a distinctly coercive quality. His virtue gave him the locus standi to dictate to others for the good of humanity. The expression he wore was that of someone who had successfully liberated his inner totalitarian.

Much may be forgiven youth. As the leader of the Chinese Communist Party, Xi Jinping, so wisely put it in a selection of his speeches and writings published by the Foreign Languages Press, everyone is young once in his life. But it is craven for older people in positions of responsibility to surrender to youth, even if the once in their lives that they were young happened to be in the 1960s.

Library of Law and Liberty, 15 March, 2016

Genetic disorder

A review of *A Troublesome Inheritance: Genes, Race and Human History* by Nicholas Wade

It is a curious paradox that those who inveigh most vehemently against race as a concept also campaign most vigorously for racial quotas by means of affirmative action. It is only a seeming paradox, however, because it is possible to acknowledge the existence of discrimination on the basis of mere physical difference without ascribing to that difference any greater taxonomic significance than its capacity to evoke the discrimination itself. Nevertheless, the very vehemence of the denial suggests some kind of whistling in the dark. And there is one further oddity to be remarked: While history is full of instances of discrimination against others, now is surely the first time in history that a group has proposed to discriminate against itself (no positive affirmation being possible without its negative corollary). Expiation for the sins of one's ancestors, rather than truth or justice, is what is sought—usually bought at someone else's expense, of course.

Nicholas Wade, the science editor of *The New York Times*, has written a book that will no doubt win him many brickbats. In it, he argues that race is a perfectly valid scientific concept and one that is supported by the latest genetic science. It is no criticism of race as a biological concept, he says, that races have no clear boundaries and that gradations between them obviously exist, for if clear boundaries existed and the races could not interbreed, they would be different species, not races. A race is a population of a single species with a cluster of genetic variants, the presence of none of which is cither a necessary or a sufficient condition of being a member of that race, but which nevertheless in aggregate gives that population distinguishing characteristics.

According to the author, there are five basic races of man, as revealed by the clustering of genetic variants: African, Caucasian (including Semitic and South Asian), East Asian, Amerindian, and Australian. There are also sub-variants within the races: for example Ashkenazi Jews, who are Caucasians but have managed for cultural reasons to maintain a genetic profile of their own. Furthermore, he says that race is of some explanatory value in world history, for the races evolved under different environmental pressures, and it is reasonable to suppose that these pressures gave rise to different psychological, as well as physical, characteristics. For example, the hypotheses that Chinese geography (unlike European) favored the emergence of a centralized state; that this necessitated the development of a powerful bureaucracy; that the kind of person who flourishes economically in such a bureaucracy, more of whose children survive to pass on their genes, is intelligent but conformist; and that therefore the Chinese are genetically more intelligent but by nature more conformist than Europeans. In point of scientific inventiveness, the effect of their conformism more than cancels out that of their superior IQ, which is why East Asian societies are still not scientific powerhouses.

Fourteen percent of the human genome, says the author, has been subject to "evolution that has been recent, copious, and regional"—not enough to divide humanity into species, but enough to make physical and mental differences between populations.

In view of the potentially explosive nature of these claims, the author is at pains to point out that no policy prescription follows from them, certainly not exploitation or genocide of one race by another. Political equality is an ethical or metaphysical concept, not one that relies for its validity on an empirical fact other than that mankind is a single species. That the concept of race has been used to justify the most hideous of crimes should no more inhibit us from examining it dispassionately as a biological and historical reality than the fact that economic egalitarianism has been used to justify crimes just as hideous should inhibit us from examining the effects of modern income distribution.

Even though the author does not crudely claim that race determines civilization, but rather that there is a constant dialectical interplay between physical environment, natural selection of advantageous physical and psychological characteristics in that environment, and the type of society to which those advantageous characteristics will give rise (an interplay that is as unending as evolution itself), I found his argument for the important historical effect of biological race on history unconvincing.

Quite early in the book, the author produces a map to illustrate the supposed interplay between genetics and culture. It is a map of Europe showing the distribution of the population with and without lactose intolerance, that is to say of the population that produces and does not produce the enzyme, lactase, that breaks down lactose, the sugar in milk. The difference between the lactose tolerant and intolerant is genetic; so, the author claims, those areas where the great majority of the population are not lactose intolerant are areas with strong dairy farming. The direction of the causal relation between the lactose tolerance and the dairy farming is not absolutely clear.

There is something very odd about this map. The further one moves in Europe from the land around the Baltic, the more prevalent lactose intolerance becomes, until in France it is very high. But France is notoriously the country that produces more varieties of cheese than the rest of the world put together, and whose production and consumption of yogurt is probably the highest in the world. (The latter is a comparatively recent development—until the 1950s yogurt was produced on a domestic scale and even then its production was not very widespread). Even allowing for the relative innocuousnesss to those with lactose intolerance of yogurt and some cheeses compared with milk, the map does not fit; and it should be remembered that there are factors other than genetic in the development of lactose intolerance. Either the map, or the point it is trying to make, is wrong.

There are other errors. The author tries to make out that the decline in the homicide rate in the western world is the result of genetic changes that gave survival advantage in new social circumstances to those who were less inclined to aggression and personal violence. These social circumstances not having yet developed in Africa, the homicide rate in the latter continent remains much higher than in Europe or the United States, the implication being that Africans are genetically more violent than the populations of Europe and the USA.

The author paints with far too broad a brush. Are there really no variations in the regions and countries of Africa, both in time and place? Is there really such continental uniformity? This was certainly not my experience of Africa, and I once travelled across it by public transport, such as it was.

Moreover, the statistics that the author uses are suspect. He says of the United States that its homicide rate is less than 2 per 100,000. The last time I looked the rate was 4.7 per 100,000—itself a very sharp decline of recent years. But a paper not long ago suggested that if the same resuscitation and surgical techniques were used as were used in 1960, the homicide rate in the United States would be five times higher than it is today, that is to say 23.5 per 100,000. The new techniques in surgery and resuscitation are unlikely to have reached much of Africa, where (the author says) the homicide rate is 10 per 100,000. In other words, either the statistics in Africa are unreliable—which in my opinion is very likely—or the statistics prove precisely the opposite of what the author wants to prove. Either way, his point is vitiated.

When our author says that western society has become much less violent, thanks (possibly) to mutations in the genes that control brain chemistry, the question naturally arises "Compared with when?" Why should we compare our current levels of violence with those of the year 1200 rather than with those of 1950, which is within the memory of many still alive? To take but one example: The number of crimes of violence in New Zealand per head of population rose by a factor of 175 between 1950 and 1999. Even allowing for possible differences in the definition and measurement of violent crime, this is a difference so startling that it is completely implausible to attribute it mainly or even partially to genetics. And, to do him justice, the author wouldn't. But this means that non-genetic factors can easily make genetic ones seem minor. In Britain, the rate of addiction to heroin in the population rose 25,000 percent between the mid-1950s and 2010. Genetics had nothing to do with this. The difference between North Korea and South—as great as that between Ukraine and Africa, say—has nothing to do with genetics.

There are many other problems with the author's thesis. He takes seriously the frequently repeated statement that hundreds of millions of Africans live on less than $1 per day. Only a moment's reflection is, or should be, necessary to establish the meaninglessness of such a statement. The notion that the average monetary value of the economic product per head of population was no different between the western world and that of, say, Africa until the Industrial Revolution, and that this fact, if it is a fact (which I very much doubt), is of any importance, is extremely doubtful. No one who visits Venice, say, and then the ruins of Great Zimbabwe—in its heyday, the acme of African cultural and material achievement for hundreds of miles around—could possibly doubt that there was an immense gulf in the intellectual achievement and sophistication of the two civilizations, even if the peasants of both lived at the same level. But the difference between Great Zimbabwe and the Masai is, or was, just as great as that between Venice and Great Zimbabwe.

By far the most interesting and convincing chapter in the book is that concerning the intellectual preeminence in the modern world of the Ashkenazi Jews. If the author's thesis applies anywhere, it is here. But he entirely omits to mention *a conditio sine qua non* of the Ashkenazi rise to preeminence, namely the European Enlightenment. And surely the name of Napoleon, not entirely worthy of respect in all other contexts, is here worth mentioning with honor. Without the Enlightenment, Ashkenazi intelligence, even if wholly genetic, could not have made so important a contribution to western civilization.

Mr. Wade is a courageous man, as is anyone who dares raise his head above the intellectual parapet; he has put his argument with force, conviction, intelligence, and clarity. He has drawn attention to possibilities that we ignore, probably as much because we prefer to ignore them as because we do not think them true on the evidence. All the same, I was not convinced: Perhaps, though not Chinese, I have the genes for conformity.

The New Criterion, May 2016

The Will to Outrage

There is no racist like an antiracist: That is because he is obsessed by race, whose actual existence as often as not he denies. He looks at the world through race-tinted spectacles, interprets every event or social phenomenon as a manifestation of racism either implicit or explicit, and in general has the soul of a born inquisitor.

That is why a recent cartoon in the Australian newspaper aroused the ire—I suspect the simulated ire, the kind of pleasantly self-righteous ire that we can all so easily work ourselves into if and when we want—of the guardians of racism purity.

The cartoon in question was by Bill Leak (who is no respecter of persons), and it showed a group of impoverished Indians sitting on the ground trying to eat some shards of smashed-up solar panels that had been given to them by the United Nations. One of them says, "It's no good, you can't eat them." Another replies, "Hang on, let me try one with a bit of mango chutney." The title of the cartoon was *"Aid à la Mode."*

It was obvious to me that this was intended as a satirical comment on the deliberations of the recent climate conference in Paris, and not on poor Indians. The cartoonist meant to imply that climate change was principally the concern of the spoiled political class of rich nations, and that efforts to reduce worldwide carbon emissions from energy consumption would not benefit the desperately poor, quite the reverse: Rather they would inhibit the breakneck industrial growth that has lifted and is lifting so many millions out of abject poverty in countries that not long ago were deeply impoverished. There is even the suspicion that rich nations want to inhibit the breakneck industrial growth not so much to save the planet as to preserve their position relative to poor nations. At the very least, the cartoon was a variation on the old English proverb that fine words butter no parsnips; but it could also plausibly be interpreted as a protest against dishonest Western moral and intellectual imperialism.

But that is not how the entrepreneurs of outrage chose to interpret it. Instead they chose to interpret it as a deliberate slur on the capacities and intelligence of ordinary Indians, who (they claimed) were depicted as so stupid and backward that they did not understand the benefits of harnessing and using solar energy. The fact that, even after so much rapid economic growth, millions of Indians would understandably be more concerned with obtaining their next meal than with the alleged fate of the planet was missed by the deliberate obtuseness of these entrepreneurs of outrage, an obtuseness motivated by their desire to "maintain their rage" (to quote a former Australian prime minister addressing his supporters on being deprived of office).

Now, I have no idea whether the harnessing of solar energy is a sensible policy for India, or whether it would merely be an opportunity for corruption and illicit private enrichment on a vast scale—or both, of course, since they are not diametrically opposed.

No one who has experienced the pollution in India or China could doubt that it is a very serious problem (as it is, to a lesser degree, in the South of France, where one can detect the pollution by the smell and gritty quality of the air as one approaches within fifty kilometers of Marseille), though whether such pollution can be dealt with only or even significantly by the use of solar energy is another question. But it is not the function of cartoonists to present a balanced view of a complex question; their method is the *reductio ad absurdum* of the side with which they disagree.

The reaction to the cartoon, however, was indicative of what one might call the will to outrage. This will precedes any object to which it might attach, and many people wait as if in ambush for something to feel angry about, pouncing on it with leopard-like joy (the leopard, so I was told in Africa, is particularly dangerous, for it kills for pleasure and not only for food).

Outrage supposedly felt on behalf of others is extremely gratifying for more than one reason. It has the appearance of selflessness, and everyone likes to feel that he is selfless. It confers moral respectability on the desire to hate or despise something or somebody, a desire never far from the human heart. It provides him who feels it the possibility of transcendent purpose, if he decides to work toward the elimination of the supposed cause of his outrage. And it may even give him a reasonably lucrative career, if he becomes a professional campaigner or politician: For there is nothing like stirring up resentment for the creation of a political clientele.

Antiracism is a perfect cause for those with free-floating outrage because it puts them automatically on the side of the angels without any need personally to sacrifice anything. You have only to accuse others of it to feel virtuous yourself. There is no defense against the accusation: The very attempt at a defense demonstrates the truth of it. As a consequence of this, it is a rhetorical weapon of enormous power that can be wielded against anybody who opposes your views. It reduces them to silence.

I once used the accusation myself in a most unscrupulous way, just to see its effect. About twenty years ago I was in the company of right-thinking people (that is to say, people who thought differently from me), among whom was an eminent human rights lawyer of impeccably internationalist outlook. She was speaking with characteristic self-righteousness about a case in which someone's newly discovered human rights had been infringed. It was shortly after the Rwandan genocide had taken place and, fed up by her moral complacency, I accused her of racism. How could she concern herself with this case, I demanded to know, when half a million people or more had just been slaughtered and the perpetrators were unpunished (as at that time they still were)? Was it because she was racist and did not consider that all those lost lives were important because they were black?

It was a preposterous thing to say, of course, completely unjust and without any foundation, and I knew it. What interested me, however, was the panic on the face of the lawyer as I accused her. It was as if I had accused St. Simeon Stylites of harboring secret sexual desires and proclivities on top of his pillar, particularly at night. She was rattled, not because what I said had any truth in it, but because it was difficult or impossible to demonstrate to the assembled company that there was none. They might therefore have thought, because there is no smoke without fire, that she was indeed not entirely free of racism. For a moment—but, of course, not for long—she feared for her auto-sanctity.

I have not used the rhetorical trick since, but something similar might be usefully employed against the detractors of Bill Leak. They are the racists, because they refuse to believe that Indians may have different interests and opinions.

Taki's Magazine, 19 December, 2015

About the Author

Theodore Dalrymple is a retired doctor who works in a British inner city hospital and prison. He has worked in Africa, the Pacific and Latin America. He has published two collections of articles (*If Symptoms Persist, and If Symptoms Still Persist*), a novel, *So Little Done: The Testament of a Serial Killer*, and a polemic on the meaning of Health scares, *Mass Listeria*. He writes for *The Spectator* in London and many newspapers. He is contributing editor of the *City Journal*, New York. His articles written for the *City Journal* have been collected in *Life at the Bottom: The Worldview That Makes the Underclass* (Ivan Dee). He has also recently published *The Intelligent Person's Guide to Health and Health Care* (Duckworth, London).

He visited Australia this year (2016) as a guest of the Centre for Independent Studies, and appeared on the ABC's Q&A.

Selected Connor Court Publications

Australian Essays
Roger Scruton
Foreword by Chris Berg
Release Date: March 2014
Paperback, 90 pages
Price: $19.95 AUD

A Duty to Offend:
Selected Essays by Brendan O'Neill
Release Date: August 2015
Paperback, 130 pages
Price: $24.95 AUD

Democracy in Decline
Steps in the Wrong Direction
James Allan
Release Date: April 2014
Paperback, 198 pages
Price: $24.95 AUD

Against the Spirit of the Age
Brian J Coman
Release Date: March 2016
Paperback, 195 pages
Price: $29.95 AUD

Studies in the Art of Rat-Catching
H.C. Barkley
With an Introduction by Brian
Coman
Release Date: March 2016
Paperback, 110 pages
Price: $19.95 AUD

More Cloak than Dagger:
One Woman's Career in Secret
Intelligence
Molly J. Sasson
Foreword by Peter Coleman AO
Release Date: August 2015
Paperback, 336 pages
Price: $29.95 AUD

Lessons in Humility:
40 Years of Teaching
Barry Dickins
Release Date: March 2013
Paperback, 270 pages
Price: $29.95 AUD